VICTOR JANZEN
Box 1509
Steinbach, Man.

# JESUS THE RELIGIOUS ULTIMATE

BY DONALD T. ROWLINGSON

*Introduction to New Testament Study*

*Jesus the Religious Ultimate*

# JESUS
# THE RELIGIOUS
# ULTIMATE

*Donald T. Rowlingson*

THE MACMILLAN COMPANY
1961   NEW YORK

First Printing

The Macmillan Company, New York
Brett-Macmillan Ltd., Galt, Ontario

Printed in the United States of America

Library of Congress catalog card number: 61-11096

# ACKNOWLEDGMENTS

❖❖❖❖❖❖❖❖   Grateful acknowledgment is made to the following publishers for permission to quote from their published works:

The Abingdon Press, for *Mahatma Gandhi: An Interpretation*, by E. Stanley Jones, copyright 1948 by the Abingdon Press.

The *Boston Globe*, for "A Salute to De Gaulle," by Walter Lippmann, April 21, 1960; The *Boston Globe* and Mark Van Doren, for "The Good Teacher," by Mark Van Doren, November 12, 1957.

The Cambridge University Press, for *The Teaching of Jesus*, by Thomas W. Manson, 1935.

The University of Chicago Press, for *The Price of Power*, by Herbert Agar, copyright 1957 by the University of Chicago.

The Christian Century Foundation, for "Why So Afraid?" by Myra Scovel, copyright 1955 by Christian Century Foundation. Reprinted by permission from the *Christian Century*.

Doubleday & Company, Inc., for *Creative Youth*, by Hughes Mearns, copyright 1925 by Doubleday & Company, Inc. Reprinted by permission of the publisher.

Harcourt, Brace and Company, for "Prayer," from *Challenge*, by Louis Untermeyer.

Harper & Brothers, for "For a Lady I Know," from *Color* by Countee Cullen, copyright 1925 by Harper & Brothers; for *Anno Domini*, by Kenneth S. Latourette, 1940; for *The Man Born to Be King*, by Dorothy L. Sayers, 1943; for *The Man Christ Jesus*, by John Knox, 1941.

Holt, Rinehart, and Winston, Inc., for *Abraham Lincoln*, by Lord Charnwood, 1917.

A. W. Lawrence, for *The Seven Pillars of Wisdom*, by T. E. Lawrence, 1938.

The Liberal Arts Press, Inc., for *Judaism: Postbiblical and Talmudic Period*, edited by Salo W. Baron and Joseph L. Blau, 1954. Reprinted by permission of the publisher, The Liberal Arts Press, Inc.

The Macmillan Company, for *Prisoner for God*, by D. Bonhoeffer, 1954, and Student Christian Movement Press, for the British edition, *Letters and Papers from Prison*; the publisher and A. & C. Black, Ltd., for *The Quest of the Historical Jesus*, by Albert Schweitzer, 1910; the publisher and Frederick C. Grant, for *Ancient Judaism and the New Testament*, by Frederick C. Grant, 1959; the publisher and George Allen & Unwin, Ltd., for *The Life of Jesus*, by Maurice Goguel, 1933; the publisher and James Nisbet and Company, Ltd., for *Jesus Son of Man*, by George S. Duncan, 1948; the publisher and St. Martin's Press, Inc., for *New Testament Background*, by C. K. Barrett, 1957; the publisher and A. P. Watt & Son and Mrs. Yeats, for "A Prayer for My Daughter," from *Selected Poems*, by W. B. Yeats, 1956.

Virgil Markham, for "Outwitted," from *The Shoes of Happiness*, by Edwin Markham, 1929, reprinted by permission of Virgil Markham.

The Pilgrim Press, for "There Is a River," by Jane Addams, from *Advance*, June 6, 1935.

Charles Scribner's Sons, for *Jesus in His Homeland*, by Sherman E. Johnson, 1957; the publisher and Student Christian Movement Press, Ltd., for *The New Being*, by Paul Tillich, 1956.

The scripture quotations used in this book are from the *Revised Standard Version of the Bible*, copyright 1946, 1952, by the Division of Christian Education of the National Council of the Churches of Christ in the United States of America, and·used by permission.

*Dedicated to L.M.R.*

# PREFACE

❖❖❖❖❖❖❖ This book is written for a certain layman I know. He has an individuality of his own, in appearance and personality, that sets him off from everyone else. At the same time he is not just one, but many. He and others like him live their individual lives in several places in which it has been my privilege over a long period of time to conduct Bible classes (notably in Atlanta and Boston). Although this layman is many, in another sense he is collectively one, because he is also a symbol. He is like certain characters in John's Gospel, both a real person and a type. For example, Nicodemus was a Jewish rabbi living in Jerusalem who sought Jesus out by night. To that extent we cannot confuse him with Nathanael or Caiaphas. At the same time he was for John a symbol of every sincere seeker after truth who hoped to have the darkness of his mind enlightened by Jesus. So my layman has many faces, yet his different faces merge into one.

What are the distinguishing characteristics of this face? It is, as has been said, the face of a layman, and this is the important fact. As a layman he is not a scholar in the field of religion in general or of

Bible study in particular. He is not like every other layman, however, because he has a more serious interest in his religion than many. He wants understanding and he is willing to think. To that end he forsakes his television program and other diversions on a week night, as well as on Sunday, to attend study groups, and he reads serious books. He is not acquainted, however, with the professional journals and the books in the field of religion written by scholars, except perhaps in a cursory way. If occasionally he tries to become better informed in this area, he is usually frustrated. The technical jargon of the professionals or their use of foreign languages, both ancient and modern, stymies him. With this occasional exception he is for all practical purposes indifferent to the debates of the scholars. His center of interest is elsewhere. It lies in the arena of pressing, practical, everyday mundane problems that crowd in upon him at home or at work. In regard to them he wants to know one thing: Is religion relevant? Does it offer guidance and inspiration in dealing with them? This is the criterion by which he judges whether discussions of religion are worth his attention. Linked with this is the demand that ideas be expressed in his idiom. This is not surprising when we remember that the most crushing indictment of the message and work of the Christian Church in our day is that they so often appear to be irrelevant in relation to the real needs and problems of mankind.

Having described the person for whom this book is written, the question naturally arises as to the reason for doing so. It may sound presumptuous, but I state it simply as a fact. He has asked me to write it. He has done this explicitly, but also indirectly through his questions as they imply his needs. This is the major reason for undertaking the work. Were it not for this, I would not have the temerity to venture into what is a very exacting task, much more exacting, in fact, than writing for one's professional colleagues. Even then it is essayed with great humility. A sense of obligation, however, forces reservations of that nature into the background. The book is also motivated by the desire to express appreciation to this layman for much that he has contributed to me. In many dynamic teaching situations it is problematical whether the teacher or the pupil learns the more from the other. I at least am conscious of a great debt to this layman, not the least part of which is the joy of association with sincere seekers after truth. If this book can in part repay that debt, it will be well worth the effort.

Looking back for a moment, it should be obvious that the distinction drawn between layman and scholar does not extend to every aspect of their relationship. The scholar also lives in the real world of pressing practical problems, and he too asks that religion be relevant. Within the context of our concern, however, the distinction still holds.

Having designated the potential reader and the reason for addressing him, it is in order to state what it is that I wish to say to him. What I have in mind to say is dictated by my understanding of his interests and needs. This in turn is governed by my efforts to keep up with what is being written and said about the specific subject, and by my attempts to evaluate it with reference to the questions and needs of my layman.

There is both an ultimate and an immediate purpose, the latter being a way of accomplishing the former. The ultimate aim is to present the challenge of Jesus to our day. I want it impressed upon the reader that Jesus is the religious ultimate, impressed upon him in such a way that he is moved to a response. Except for a few observations in the concluding chapter, however, this is not done directly. Beyond that final chapter there is no intention of making specific the application of Jesus' ideas and meaning to current issues. That is left to the reader, as ultimately it must be.

My immediate and specific concern is with the foundation upon which this practical superstructure of application is reared. The chief interest of the book is to portray Jesus in his native habitat many years ago. The fundamental assumption behind this procedure is that, before we can know the ways in which Jesus is relevant today, we must see him realistically in his own day. Allied with this is the further assumption that this is the only way in which we can come to know him intimately enough to understand the nature of his challenge. To by-pass this foundational aspect of the total issue, in a more direct and less arduous effort to learn what Jesus may mean to us, is like trying to grow fruit from trees suspended in the air. Certain thinkers today are making that mistake. They offer us a disembodied Christ or an abstract idea instead of a person. In this type of thought Christ is an x, as one writer has well expressed it. The refutation of this line of thought appears to me of great importance. This is the final and compelling reason for dealing with the subject along the lines that have been indicated.

An analogy may be in order for the sake of emphasizing the validity of the point of view I assume. I find Lincoln a constant source of light and inspiration, but this is due to the fact that I see him rising to heroic stature in real-life situations. I know no other way by means of which he can impress his character upon me. Nor do I know any other way than that by means of which Jesus can challenge me. Dietrich Bonhoeffer, a martyr under the Nazis, was right when he wrote to his parents in August, 1944, "We must persevere in quiet meditation on the life, sayings, deeds, sufferings and death of Jesus in order to learn what God promises and what he fulfills."

This still does not explain why one needs to write a book on the subject. Why not simply study the Gospels? The question has merit, and it should not be dismissed with a wave of the hand. Much can be gained by serious reading and meditation in this respect. In fact it is indispensable. One does not need books about Jesus in order to learn some very important things. There is a self-authenticating impression of Jesus in the Gospels, going to the heart of his mind and spirit, which no sensitive spirit can miss. One does not need to be a scholar to recognize it and to feel its impact. The scholar can neither create it nor destroy it. There it stands, like Mount Everest, awesome and challenging, and offering as well light and power to the pure in heart. If we have eyes to see, we behold its glory without the aid of the scholars. It thrusts itself upon us as authentic and real.

However, the scholar can help us to sharpen and refine the impressions we get by reading. He can do this in several ways, the most important of which is to inform us of what Jesus' contemporaries were thinking and doing. This enables us to picture Jesus realistically against his background, and thus to understand him better and to appreciate with greater insight the marvel of his accomplishment. This fact is pertinent to the question as to why a book about Jesus may add something to the study of the Gospels. It indicates the prevailing emphasis of the following pages. To bring some of the information and insight which the scholars contribute to bear upon features of the Gospel portraits, so that more vividly we may comprehend Jesus and his meaning, is my interest. To that end it is not necessary to attempt an exhaustive textbook or to debate every moot point. If a point of view and a general impression can be created which contain authentic notes—that will suffice.

The book is organized with all these elements of motivation in mind. The ultimate objective finds expression mainly in the concluding chapter, with Chapter I preparing the way. The specific purpose is fulfilled in Chapters I through V. Attention is concentrated upon the meaning God had for Jesus. This was the unique, as well as the all-consuming, feature of his thought, as it was of the Judaism in which he was reared. By way of orientation the opening chapter sets our feet upon the ground of previous study of the subject. This is important to the whole, because it involves the crucial question of presuppositions. Chapter II deals with the subject of Jesus' uniqueness with reference to Judaism, his personal relationship to God being the crux of the matter. The three chapters that follow concentrate upon Jesus' ideas of God. The chapter headings are provided by the three aspects of God's nature and functioning that characterized ancient Jewish thought: "The Creator," "The Sovereign," "The Redeemer." Under each heading the Jewish background and Jesus' reactions to it will be described and evaluated. We shall see in each chapter that Jesus took certain conceptions for granted at the same time that he qualified or challenged others. The emphases that arise in his teaching and that are reflected in his actions constitute the unique contribution he made. By grasping these emphases clearly we come to understand his accomplishment, and thus his relevance for our time.

Because of the readers to whom this book is addressed, no effort is made, beyond copyright acknowledgments, to specify indebtedness for assistance in its composition. Any informed reader will be able to identify the springs from which I have quenched my thirst, and others will not care. I can only say that I am fully conscious of how much I owe to many, within and without the circle of my colleagues in theological education, which I acknowledge with the deepest gratitude.

D. T. R.

Winchester, Massachusetts
December 1, 1960

# CONTENTS

# I

## THE LESSONS OF THE
## PAST AND THEIR BEARING
## UPON PRESUPPOSITIONS

✛✛✛✛✛✛ Every subject of study, like every individual and every social group, has a past. It has a history. This constitutes a heritage upon which our feet are planted as we think and work in the present. It is the part of wisdom to know this heritage well. It conditions much of the present and it can teach us to avoid mistakes. It can give us data upon the basis of which to form valid presuppositions. It is this that concerns us here. Our interest centers in that segment of the past that involves the influence of Jesus and the reactions of men to him. We are interested in it primarily with reference to the presuppositions upon the basis of which we think about Jesus and his meaning. We shall consider first the nature of presuppositions, and then specific ways in which the past influences presuppositions relative to our subject.

Everything we undertake rests upon certain antecedents of thought that we largely take for granted. This applies equally to the most practical and to the most theoretical of our enterprises. For example, we set the alarm clock and go to sleep. Unless we have reason to suspect erratic behavior on its part, we take for granted that its disconcerting sound will awaken us in the morning. But in this simple

operation we assume much more than that. We assume that the earth
will continue to rotate regularly upon its axis and that every other
related feature of the entire universe will continue in equilibrium.
All this we presuppose when we believe that the conditions of our
awakening tomorrow will be the same as they were yesterday. This
simple illustration typifies what happens in everything we think and
do. The same conditions are as evident in the baking of a cake as in
the launching of a rocket, in playing baseball as in making astro-
nomical calculations. We would be paralyzed both in thought and
action without presuppositions of some kind. They are as inevitable
as taxes!

It is obvious that, if we are to experience desirable results in our
planning and our work, our presuppositions must be sound. This
applies particularly to the area in which we are working, the realm
of historical study. In this area the conclusions one reaches are irrevocably influenced, and often determined, by what is presupposed.
This should become clear as we proceed.

The important distinction to be made in this field is that between a presupposition based upon evidence and one rooted in
a biased or wishful desire that goes against existing evidence. Illustrations of the latter are not hard to find in the field of Bible study.
There is the assumption, for example, that the Bible was in some
mysterious way dictated by God word for word, including punctua-
tion marks, the human writers being but robot "pens" in his hand.
This has no support in evidence. The Bible itself makes no such claim.
Every shred of valid evidence implies that the books of the Bible were
composed by the same human means as any other. This does not in-
validate its religious truth. It has to do only with a method of composition. Another equally fallacious premise is that which holds that
the scientific views of Genesis represent God's views. Modern science completely shatters such an assumption. On a higher level there
is the type of presupposition that is a half-truth, as when it is said
that "the Bible centers in Christ." As an expression of faith, it may
have merit, although it is not accurately expressed. Historically viewed,
this cannot be claimed for the Old Testament. The Old Testament
does not center in Christ at all; it centers in the history of Israel.
If it is meant that the Old Testament is background, even prepara-
tion, for Christ, it should be so stated. As it stands it is an unwarranted generalization.

Rational presuppositions, on the other hand, are consistent with all the available evidence. With regard to the composition of the Bible, for instance, full value will be given to the evidence of the human element. Every other issue will be similarly judged, avoiding the wishful thinking that ignores or denies factual data bearing upon it.

This distinction between different types of presuppositions should not be confused with the distinction between faith and evidence. Faith is present in every presupposition, whether it be a valid or an invalid one, although with regard to an invalid one the faith attitude should more properly be labeled credulity. On the positive side, the scientist has faith in the uniformity of nature. This presupposition is an act of faith simply because the complete evidence to verify it is not observable. But it grows out of, and is consistent with, as much of the evidence as can be observed. It is at least never contradicted by any known fact. There are those, on the other hand, who still presuppose that the earth is flat. This is an act of faith too, but it is held in the face of evidence that makes it obsolete. Both the scientist and his detractor have faith in an unprovable premise, but the one is intelligent while the other is not. The historian deals with data different from those of natural science, but he must also make an assertion of faith, and he has the same alternatives of an informed or an uninformed decision.

Having drawn the distinction between a rational and an irrational, a valid and an invalid, presupposition, we are now prepared to see how this applies specifically to our field of study. As has been said, the purpose is to state a series of presuppositions that undergird our study as they are taught us by the lessons of the past.

There are two categories to be considered. The first consists of certain general lessons that have to do with the impact of Jesus upon the generations subsequent to his earthly life. The second consists of specific lessons we learn from the efforts that have gone into the historical study of his life and thought since the late eighteenth century.

## GENERAL LESSONS

Two of these lessons will concern us in this section. The first deals with the value of Jesus for religion. The second raises the question

of how, or in what particular ways, he is significant. Both issues are
oriented toward our situation today.

### 1. *Jesus Is the Religious Ultimate*

The word "religious" distinguishes the area in which Jesus makes
his contribution from that of "scientific" or "political" or "literary" or
even "theological." The point of the contrast between religion and
theology is that Jesus makes his impact far more in the realm of our
need of salvation, having to do with our experience, than in that of
our need to explain him, having to do primarily with our mind. How
he is able to save men, theologically formulated, is for the moment at
least less important than the fact of his power. The term "ultimate"
implies a superiority about Jesus with reference to man's quest for
salvation that places him above every other Saviour. In the broadest
terms, it means that Jesus is the definitive guide to the meaning of our
existence and also the chief inspiration to rise to its challenge and possibilities. This is not to say that he is the only one through whom
God has revealed and mediated his redemption, but only that he is
unequaled by any other.

This is obviously an assertion of faith, a value judgment. At the
same time it is consistent with evidence. It is a judgment that grows
out of the actual experience of many people over the centuries. Every
truly Christian confession of faith has this as its basic affirmation. It
may be said as simply as it was by Peter: "Lord, to whom shall we go?
You have the words of eternal life." Or it may take the more complex
and obscure form of the Nicene Creed. Beyond the intellectual response is the whole realm of emotional and imaginative reaction to
Jesus in poetry, drama, art, and music. In whatever form, the claim
is made on the basis of experience that Jesus, above all others, answers
the deepest questions life poses, and as a result provides salvation most
satisfactorily.

There is also a more objective kind of evidence. It is summed up
in the words of a modern Church historian: "Measured by its fruits
in the human race that short life has been the most influential ever
lived on this planet. . . . Because of it mankind is better off than it
could possibly have been without it." A Khrushchev may scoff at such
an idea, and more serious minds may question it, but it stands in the

face of all the evidence. Were it not for this evidence, it would be impossible to believe that a crucified criminal in first century Palestine could accomplish in history what Jesus has. It would be too fantastic to credit. The important point here is the beneficent effect Jesus has demonstrably had, when his spirit has actually been caught and reproduced. It is not his fault that his Church has in many ways denied him and betrayed him. Revivals of his spirit within the Church, in large or small dimensions, always work for good.

In the light of this record it is reasonable to assume that what Jesus has meant to many he can mean to all. He has something to offer non-Christians, as Gandhi learned, and he can reinvigorate professing Christians, leading them to deeper levels of understanding and of more discriminating and more dedicated loyalty. It is important, with that in view, that both the Christian and the non-Christian give him a chance.

This is particularly relevant to the current debate with respect to the relationship between Christianity and other world religions. On the one side are those who stress the exclusiveness and the particularity of the Christian faith. They assert that the non-Christian must be converted to Christianity in one of its institutional expressions with reference to a set of beliefs about Jesus Christ. On the other side are those who claim that exclusiveness must be tempered in the direction of a vital universalism. They stress the basic religious and ethical convictions of the Christian faith, and see the true spirit of Jesus being expressed in every man who offers himself to the absolute love of God and genuine love of neighbor, whatever his formal confession in theological and ecclesiastical terms. We make no effort here to arbitrate this issue. We content ourselves with pointing out that, if Jesus is the religious ultimate, in some way or other something is offered in him that man cannot find elsewhere, at least in the same measure or abundance. We call attention too to the crucial nature of this question in a world in which the old divisions and parochialisms are collapsing, with much travail, in the face of a new world being born. The issue cannot be avoided in the sphere of religion, since at root it is religious in nature. These thoughts indicate the relevance of the idea that Jesus is the religious ultimate. In assuming this, we are not dealing with an academic issue. We are rather caught up in the struggle of vital issues upon the solution of which humanity's existence depends.

## 2. The Historical Jesus Is Vital to Faith

The expression "Historical Jesus" needs explaining. It is a term used by scholars to differentiate between the earthly existence of Jesus and his subsequent influence in the faith and experience of his followers. For the latter experience they use the term "Christ of Faith." It is a rather unfortunate division of thought, since there is but one Jesus. Yet it does coincide with the reality of Jesus' impact upon men. There was a person named Jesus who lived in ancient Palestine and who was crucified under Pilate. There is also the person who, as an exalted heavenly being, influenced men after his death. These are but different aspects of one person, yet they are real and significant differences.

Under the designation "Christ of Faith" are to be included theological interpretations of his person and significance, as well as direct contact with him in the form of resurrection appearances and mystical experience. Within the New Testament both aspects of Jesus appear, usually interwoven with each other. A statement of Paul may serve as a simple illustration. On one occasion he wrote to the Corinthians (I Cor. 15:3): "I delivered to you . . . that Christ died for our sins in accordance with the scriptures." Three facets of this statement should be distinguished from each other.

The first is a vital statistic, the fact of the death of Jesus. This was a fact of public observation open to everyone who cared to investigate the matter.

The other two facets, however, are interpretations of the significance of his death that were obvious only to disciples of Jesus, and were disbelieved by others. The first of these is the conviction that he died "for our sins," that is, for our redemption. This may have been an actual fact in the sense that it expressed Jesus' intention in going to the cross and also in the redemptive significance his death had for many. It was not, however, a vital statistic like the actual ending of his life, obvious to everyone. It was Christian interpretation, and as such in the realm of the Christ of Faith rather than in that of the Historical Jesus.

The other item is the idea that he died "in accordance with the scriptures." This is different from both of the preceding items in the statement. Like the statement about the redemptive significance of Jesus' death, it is interpretation. Unlike it, it does not rest upon something experienced, but wholly upon speculation. It was a theory about the Hebrew scriptures to the effect that Jesus had been predicted, that details of his career and his meaning for faith had been envisaged by Hebrew piety before he was born. On a deeper level it signified that his death had not been a miscarriage of justice, but according to God's plan. The last of these meanings may well be true, but the theory as such cannot be sustained in the face of our knowledge of the way in which the Old Testament originated. Thus the early Christians were mistaken in seeking to explain the significance of Jesus by that method. However, it too was an aspect of what we mean by the "Christ of Faith."

The point of all this is that both fact, in nature like a vital statistic, and interpretation (of different kinds) exist side by side, or are interlaced, in the New Testament picture of Jesus. Or, the Historical Jesus and the Christ of Faith exist together.

This is just as true of the Gospels as of other New Testament books. There is here a greater degree of interest in his teachings and actions (the Historical Jesus) than elsewhere, but the facts of his life and thought are set within the context of interpretations of his significance (the Christ of Faith). John makes this quite evident in a very deliberate way at the end of Chapter 20. He says that his purpose is to portray an exalted Jesus in such a way that his readers will be moved to believe in him as Son of God, and thus experience eternal life in his name. Mark is more subtle but no less emphatic when his opening sentence describes his writing as "The beginning of the gospel of Jesus Christ, the Son of God." That is, he is writing the story of the unique Son of God, a historical person with transcendental significance, in the interests of evangelization. The very word "gospel" implies the redemptive significance of Jesus who is Christ and Son of God. The interpretative element is more subtle in the first three Gospels than in John, but it is nonetheless present. Wherever we meet Jesus in the New Testament, within or without the Gospels, we confront a glorified human being who has definitive significance for faith.

The scholars employ another term besides the "Christ of Faith" to express this aspect of the New Testament view. We shall avoid its use because of its technical nature, but it is well to become acquainted with it in passing. It is *kerygma,* a Greek word meaning "preaching," "proclamation," "affirmation of faith," in contrast with *didache,* or "teaching." The New Testament Kerygma is its proclamation of the significance of Jesus as revealer of God and mediator of his salvation, which challenges us to decision for or against him.

The relevance of this to our concern with presuppositions arises from the claim some theologians are making today for the Kerygma. They are insisting that it is (almost) exclusively in the Kerygma that we are to look for God's revelation of himself through Jesus. By this they mean that the Historical Jesus is unimportant beyond the fact that he did live and die. By implication some who take this position question even that. They appear to believe that we do not need a historical person, that an idea as such will do. Without going to such extremes, however, the main thought here is that we learn practically nothing about God's Word for us in what Jesus may actually have said and done while he was on earth.

It is against this position that this second presupposition is directed. It is believed that to attribute such exclusiveness to the Kerygma, the Christ of Faith, in the New Testament fails at two points. It is not consistent with the Bible's view of itself, especially with its conception of the nature of revelation. It gives a one-sided emphasis to what in reality has two sides, both Historical Jesus and Christ of Faith, with both sides held in a unity. Furthermore, it violates the dictates of common sense. Common sense in this respect means something more profound than the superficial type of observation that looks only at the surface of things. It means that which makes sense, even though it may not be so common.

Consider first the nature of the Bible's view of revelation. The Bible contains little, if any, pure history. It contains historical events interpreted to religious ends in accordance with a religious philosophy of history. The story of Moses, for example, is related in such a way as to stimulate faith in the Election and divine destiny of Israel. It is interpretation, containing much that is legendary. However, the interpretation arises from events that actually occurred. The basic "facts" are not invented, however much they may be colored or distorted, as they are in much pagan mythology. This is the case as well with New Testament interpretations of Jesus. It is taken for granted that he did and said certain things in history and that his history is a prerequisite to the meaning he came to have. This is as true of Paul as of Mark. Paul's idea that Jesus descended from heaven to earth for the sake of man's salvation would mean nothing without the fact of the death of Jesus that lies at its heart. Mark's theory of Jesus' cosmic significance, which he sees as made manifest in his casting of demons out of emotionally disturbed people, rests upon the fact that Jesus did cure such deranged spirits.

Simply put, the New Testament idea of revelation, consistent with the Old Testament, is that of Incarnation (in the form of flesh or in genuine human form). God expressed himself, that is, in what Jesus said and did on earth, and not only later in the form of the Resurrection and the giving of the Spirit. Whatever he may have done later, he began with the Word made flesh, and without that there could have been no second stage, no Christ of Faith. The meaning of the Christ of Faith is determined by the Historical Jesus, even though the true significance of the latter may be given in the former. In other words, Historical Jesus and Christ of Faith are the same in fundamental respects, no matter what the distinction they serve to define in theology and in religious experience. At least this much is evident. If we are to understand the challenge of Jesus to faith we must give content to the Christ of Faith (or Kerygma) by means of knowledge of Jesus' earthly career. Here only can we observe in clear-cut reality the Word made flesh.

Common sense reinforces this verdict of scripture. Consider the analogy of Lincoln. We do not need to labor the differences between the impact of Lincoln and that of Jesus following their respective deaths. No one claims that Lincoln rose from the dead or that he founded a religion. To emphasize these differences, however, is to obscure the similarities between them with respect to their subsequent influence. There is an image of Lincoln which persists in memory, including legend as well as fact, and he does continue to exert a mighty influence upon many. The form in which he does so is that of a memory of his earthly life, not of some imaginary event. What inspires us is a concrete memory of his character, which expressed itself, as it grew, in insight and courage in facing life's contingencies. We recall a Second Inaugural Address, for example, and in it a magnanimity toward the South that, looking back to the circumstances in which it appeared, seems almost superhuman. We are inspired, that is to say, by a life.

When we turn in the direction of Jesus, common sense and experience teach us that the same conditions hold true. What he had to reveal about the nature of God he manifested in actual teaching and in realistic acting within a historical context. It is this that made the experiences of his exalted presence something more than vague emotional upheavals. If it is not true that the challenge of Jesus lies fundamentally in what we observe of him during his life on earth, then we have no sure ground upon which to base our faith in him. This is what the New Testament itself implies, especially in the Gospels, and it is what experience and common sense confirm.

We are not saying that we may not need more than this for the fullest experience of Christian salvation. We are only insisting that we cannot do with less, any more than one can erect the superstructure of a building without a foundation, or grow trees without roots. It may be said that some, like Luther, came to Jesus by way of the Kerygma in Paul rather than directly through the Gospels. That is certainly true. There are many avenues to the central shrine. However, soon or late, whatever the avenue of approach, Jesus must be ·confronted in his individuality in a concrete way if we are to be sure that we are dealing with *him* rather than with a figment of the imagination. If not, how can we ever be sure that it is *Jesus* whom we confront? The answer is that we can't.


## SPECIFIC LESSONS

The study of Jesus in the Gospels by scientific means, by historical method, that is, has been going on since Reimarus initiated the procedure in 1778. The most significant impetus to the development in its early stages, however, was given by David Friedrich Strauss when his Life of Jesus was published in 1835. Since then the study of the Gospels has produced an avalanche of literature concerned with every minute detail of their interrelationships and meaning. The vital element in all this has been the passion to discover the "Real Jesus," Jesus as he actually was on earth. The results confront us today with a manifold variety of interpretations. Our interest in this arises from one of the three necessities of adequate analysis of any subject that has a history. That is to be familiar with the work of others before us and around us. In formulating our presuppositions we must take all this into account. Out of this effort come the specific lessons the past teaches us relative to our subject.

We shall confine our attention to two of these lessons under this heading. Both are crucial and both are pertinent to debate going on at the present time among the scholars. The first concerns our ability to come to grips with the Historical Jesus, the Real Jesus. Can we really find him underneath the layers of interpretation with which his earthly career is encrusted in the Gospels? We can see the ways in which the early Christians viewed him, but can we really see him as he was? The second item deals with proper method and point of view in our efforts to reconstruct his life and thought. This has to do directly with that which we are seeking to accomplish in this whole chapter, that is, determine valid presuppositions.

## 1. We Can Know the Historical Jesus

The thought of certain scholars is dominated by an extreme skepticism with regard to our ability to recover authentic reminiscences of Jesus. They insist that the Gospel reports are too colored, too distorted, by Jesus' first interpreters to make that possible. We can get back to his earliest interpreters, but we cannot get to him. This is a reflection within the area of our interest of a skeptical strain of thought that has a much wider context. Much of philosophy and the writing of history during the last one hundred years has moved in this mood. This has been due largely to the prestige of the natural sciences. The ambition to be "scientific" invaded the fields of the humanities and religion, often with very unfortunate results. Fortunately, at the present time the pendulum is swinging the other way. The limitations of science in historical studies, as well as its very important contributions, are more clearly discerned, with the result that the prevailing skepticism of many of our immediate predecessors is being dissipated. Our treatment will seek to give the pendulum a push in what we consider to be the right direction.

The fact of the matter is that the Gospels are adequate sources of knowledge of Jesus as he really was. That is, they tell us all that we

need to know in order to make an intelligent decision regarding Jesus'
challenge to faith. We do not need to labor the point that there is
much that we should like to know about Jesus which they do not
tell us. There are gaps in the story, especially with regard to his life
prior to the beginning of his public ministry. Many interesting details,
such as the color of Jesus' eyes, are missing. How much difference it
would make if we had a tape recording of the tone and quality of
his voice! It would be very helpful to have accurate medical diagnoses
of the various ailments he is reported to have cured. It would be helpful to be certain of the exact sequence of events in his career, with the
exact dates of his birth and death, none of which, beyond certain
general features, do we possess. And the list could be extended.

But none of this really makes any great difference beyond the
satisfaction of historical curiosity. We know enough for our religious
interests to be met. We know the essential ingredients of his thought
and something of the quality of his dedication to his mission. We
sense his individuality and the startling and amazing way in which he
stood out from his contemporaries. We have enough information
to picture him as a concrete and dynamic individual, and, as a result,
to understand the true nature of his challenge and of what he offers
mankind. We are sufficiently informed to be able to give a satisfactory
answer to the most important question of all, that is, of what he accomplished to produce the impact upon mankind that he has. Why
should we ask for more?

We must of course take seriously the fact that the Gospel records
are colored and distorted. We must be ready to acknowledge that even
the reported words of Jesus have in many instances been created by
early Christians. We must recognize that in this fashion ideas have
been attributed to Jesus that were not his. This, and much more, is
obvious. The problems here are difficult and complex, and their solution demands the skill of trained scholars. But this should not be
exaggerated, since there is another side to the shield. We are dealing
with records that originated very closely in time to the events they
embody, and much of the material came from eyewitnesses. Only an
arbitrarily skeptical spirit can deny the significance of this for our
confidence in the essential reliability of the portraits.

There is a self-authenticating quality about the Gospels that goes far to buttress this confidence. It is as immediately available to the discerning layman as to the scholar. The scholar has a role to fulfill in Gospel study that cannot be minimized, but he does not have a monopoly upon the capacity to sense this prescientific impression the Gospels make upon the open-minded reader. This impression of authenticity does not concern details of the records, but only certain general features. With regard to many details we are at sea, and scholarly judgment fluctuates in the realm of probabilities. In outstanding general ways, however, the records bear testimony to certainties that are not affected by the opinions of the scholars. Selected fundamental characteristics of Jesus stand out so boldly and so strikingly that only the blind can fail to see them. They are obviously true simply because they could not have been invented. They thrust themselves upon the unprejudiced and the sympathetic reader. What is more, they are not confined to what are called the major and most authentic sources of the Gospels. They exist in every layer of the Gospel tradition, in secondary and legendary elements as well as in primary data. They combine to confront us with a tremendous individual of unique proportions. This prescientific impression, not at all dependent upon the work of the historical scholar, stares us in the face when we confront the Gospels with purity of heart. We have every reason to believe that in these basic and general features of the Gospel portraits we see the Historical Jesus.

With respect to this aspect of the subject, the scholar has no advantage over the layman. They both stand on the same ground. On the other hand, we must not sell the scholar short. His training does permit him to make a contribution that cannot be made by anyone else. He can refine and sharpen many features of the structural framework that is given, so as to make more realistic our understanding of Jesus. His knowledge of the ancient languages Jesus spoke and in which the records were written contributes many valuable insights. His knowledge of the literary features of the Gospels can help. Above all, his orientation in the ancient setting of Jesus' life is invaluable. Knowing the Judaism in which Jesus was born and reared, as well as the wider world of which Judaism was but one segment, he is in a position to cast light upon the meaning of what Jesus said and did. This is prerequisite to full understanding and appreciation of Jesus.

As we proceed we shall have occasion to acknowledge the indispensable contributions the scholars make to our study.*

For the moment we are content to state the facets of a presupposition. That Jesus can be known, at least in certain general ways, to the extent that we need to know him is what matters. Of this we can be confident.

## 2. Correct Method and a Valid Point of View Are Crucial

This is what is being said in this whole chapter, but we need to be more specific about two facets of the total question. Granting that Jesus can be known, how do we go about the task of getting acquainted with him? More particularly, what is required in terms of method of study and point of view? As we concentrate upon the Gospels, we can vitiate the results by wrong methodology and an inadequate point of view. If the given impressions of the Gospels are to make their full impact upon us, we must be concerned about these matters.

We concern ourselves with the question of method. There is only one legitimate method of studying the past in an effort to reconstruct events and the biography of the individuals who participated in them. This applies to the study of Jesus just as much as to anyone else. The method goes under the general heading of "historical." This means the determination by generally accepted criteria to find out what a person in the past actually said or wrote, and to give his words the meanings that in his setting he intended them to have. The words may be those of a writer, such as Mark and the other Evangelists or Paul, or those of a speaker or teacher, as Jesus. The opposite of this method is to read into the text the meanings we prefer to find there without taking the pains involved in the other method. With reference to interpretation, two technical words describe this difference. *Exegesis* (to draw out) is to permit the writer's meanings to emerge naturally from what he says as we seek all the help we can get from various sources to give us understanding. *Eisegesis* (to lead in) is to introduce into our conception of the words of the text anything that our imagination or bias wishes. The former has its feet planted in the setting of the original, the latter in the modern day. This latter

* Cf. books listed at the end for information on the background of Jesus.

point of view causes "modernization" of the text, as when knowledge of Darwinian evolution is assumed on the part of a first century writer who could not possibly have had the slightest inkling of it.

The reasons for the latter procedure are not difficult to discern. We want our ideas or prejudices confirmed by the Bible. Because we do, misinterpretations of the Bible clutter up the history of Christianity and still reign in many quarters. Another reason is that we do not know any better. This is one reason for this exposition: that we may learn. There is another reason that places blame upon no one. It is the sheer impossibility of knowing all that one must know adequately to fulfill that which is required. If one were to know everything that complete application or historical procedures demands, he would have to be a master of several fields of study all at once. There are few, if any, scholars today who can meet that test. The subject matter is so vast and so complex that a scholar does very well if he masters one segment of it. Just as in the field of the natural sciences the historical scholar is a specialist who collaborates with other specialists in order to fulfill the aims of historical reconstruction. If the scholar is so limited, where does that leave the layman? It leaves him very dependent for some things upon a combination of scholars no single one of whom can give him a comprehensive view of things.

When we have granted this difficulty, the fact still remains that there is much that the layman can do with reference to his method of Bible study. He can at least learn the difference between valid historical method and other methods. He can strive to interpret the Bible by means of exegesis rather than eisegesis. He can discipline his imagination and his bias to this end. And, if he is willing to study, he can gain enough insight from the scholars to make his study fruitful. The fact of the complexity of historical study cannot be ignored. On the other hand, it may be used as a means of escape from much that can be done.

What really need emphasis with regard to historical method are two prerequisites that express themselves in an attitude of mind. Every individual, be he scholar or layman, can achieve them, and they are actually the ingredients that distinguish the truly historical spirit from its counterfeits. One of these is an open mind, the refusal to prejudge the results of an investigation until all the evidence is in. This is the mind purged of bias, so far as possible, especially of prejudices of an arbitrary nature. Or, it is the mind that tries to understand and purify its presuppositions. This is the "scientific" aspect of historical method. It is indispensable and fundamental.

The second prerequisite is just as important in combination with the former. It is one that is all too often ignored by those who pride themselves upon their "scientific" and objective attitude. It is sympathy with the subject of study. It is the opposite of indifference, which is often confused with objectivity. Indifference may simply be an insensitivity that is blind. Some things cannot be per-ceived, their deeper meanings grasped, without sympathy or even faith.

With reference to the study of Jesus, the quality of sympathy we have in mind is not necessarily that of complete commitment to him. Ultimately it may mean that, but it has a broader base. It is something less exclusive. In minimum terms it is the ability to appreciate greatness when we confront it. It is the capacity that arises from experience to respond to the deeper levels of the human spirit. It is a purity of heart that intuitively sees meanings in events and in persons. In the case of Jesus, as of other great persons, it is an appreciative response to the impact he has made upon mankind. This quality of sympathy should predispose us to come to the Gospels with the expectation of finding causes sufficient to explain the influence Jesus has had. We should take it for granted that in his life he did something in such a unique and outstanding way that the actual result history records could not have been otherwise. This is not to say that we should invent or create what is not in the records. We speak only of an attitude of mind. Carrying it further, when we do find in the Gospels evidences of marked originality, as we do, we should assume without any question that we are in the presence of reality, historical reality. We should take it for granted that we have put our finger upon that which is most authentic in the reports.

When the quality of sympathy joins with a truly open mind, we shall be able adequately to see the Historical Jesus. We shall at least avoid the kind of distorted portraiture that seizes upon an inferior aspect of the record as the key to the whole. We shall interpret the lesser by the greater, the inferior by the superior, and thus arrive at a reasonably acceptable result.

This is still not enough with reference to a point of view. We have to presuppose something about the nature of Jesus. There is danger "genius" is in many ways watered down in our day so that it means nothing very distinctive. Taken in its purest and profoundest meaning, however, it is adequate. Furthermore, it can be construed within the context of a definition of "supernatural" that makes sense to modern thought.

To explain Jesus by means of the category of genius is to say that he exerted an inexplicable creative influence upon the social factors that conditioned him in the period of ancient Judaism. It is to say of him what we mean when we speak of the intellectual genius of Shakespeare or the musical genius of Beethoven. The only difference is the conditioning adjective. In the case of Jesus it was *religious* genius as compared with intellectual or musical genius. This is not fully to explain Jesus. The term "genius" is a designation for an ultimate category of personality. It is an end point. It is not an explanation, but a description. The fact of genius can only be observed and its manifestations described. There is a profound mystery about it that abides, and defies efforts to elucidate its component parts. It is a manifestation of the irrational in human beings and in human history.

This can be conceived within the framework of a truly "supernatural" conception of Jesus. In its fundamental connotations "supernatural" is an inclusive term. It designates the influence of the divine in human existence, in whatever form it may take. In that sense, on a theistic view, genius is as much a manifestation of God's activity as is the Word of John's Gospel. They represent simply two different ways of trying to define the same thing. There is no reason in the world why traditionalists in religion should be permitted to monopolize the word "supernatural." The issue has very little to do in reality with an alleged conflict between natural and supernatural conceptions of Jesus. It is a question of whether we are to explain Jesus by means of archaic and obsolete formulas, however much they have in the past served the interests of piety, or by conceptions relevant to our world of thought. This is but one part of the total issue of the relevance of the Church to the real needs of people in the twentieth century. Within that context there is no way that is superior to the idea of genius to account for Jesus' accomplishment.

In the determination to bring our conceptions of Jesus up to date we are reminded that that was exactly what John was trying to when he used the idea of the Word of God in his Gospel. He w

here of arguing in a circle, since the impressions of the Gospels them
selves are part of the data for thinking about the question. However
the data go beyond what can be observed in the Gospels, and the pas
study of Jesus makes it evident that the question stands in its ow
right. In essence the problem is to account for his achievement. Be
yond what we can see in his teachings and actions, what is involved
There are only two alternatives. They cannot be combined, althoug
some try to do so. Either Jesus was a supernatural being or he was
genuine human being. Either he had personal equipment beyon
the range of normal humanity or he thought and acted under th
conditions common to every human being. He was either "tempte
in all points as we are" or not at all.

The New Testament is not entirely consistent in its testimony o
this point. Certain speculative propositions tend to qualify the gen
ineness of his humanity. This is true of the doctrine of virgin birt
and the idea of his preexistence implied in Paul and John. At the sam
time it is generally assumed that he was genuinely a human bein
among other human beings. In the second century Christian orth
doxy repudiated the claims of a type of thought called Gnosticism
the effect that a sharp distinction was to be drawn between the huma
and the divine elements in Jesus. Orthodox doctrine insisted on th
reality and the genuineness of both elements. This remained the orth
dox view down through the period of the formation of the cree
There is an ambiguity here that speculative thought cannot solv
What the creeds tried to preserve was the conviction that, religious
speaking, Jesus had the full value of God. They asserted that Jes
was completely sufficient for salvation because he embodied Go
grace and power completely. At the same time they insisted that th
was accomplished in the form of an Incarnation, that is, in the fle
—in a truly human manner.

We cannot solve the question in our time by means of cree
formulations that arose in a thought-world quite different from
own. We must appeal to categories of thought meaningful to
Nor can we have it both ways. That is, we cannot conceive of Je
as both supernatural and as genuinely human. We cannot do t
unless we can find some form of thought that permits us to def
"supernatural" in such a way that a genuine human being can be
conceived. There is such a category. It is that of genius. The te

ing to help his readers comprehend the meaning of Jesus in terms that had relevance to their thought in an environment quite different from that in which Jesus had done his thinking. John thought it was a prerequisite for grasping and being moved by Jesus' power to save. We are reminded too that John's interpretation was resisted as too novel and too "modern" by those who had been brought up on the conceptions of the first three Gospels. It is a little difficult now to appreciate the fact that, when it first appeared, John's Gospel seemed to be destroying the faith. This at least has a lesson for us. We seek to accomplish no more than John did, no more in fact than did every succeeding wave of thinkers who have over the centuries sought to make Jesus intelligible.

The category of genius is not wholly adequate, but it is not less adequate than any other explanation, ancient or modern. No explanation is completely adequate, simply because no great man, let alone Jesus, can ever be fully explained. At least the conception of genius preserves his mystery at the same time that it does so in a form of thought that makes contact with conceptions meaningful to our day. The latter is more than can be said for most ancient formulations. Finally, this manner of accounting for the inexplicable in Jesus offers an intelligible means by which to implement the sympathy for the subject of study that is a prerequisite of historical method.

These then are the presuppositions of our study of Jesus. They will obviously influence the judgments passed and the conclusions reached in the ensuing pages. The reader must judge for himself whether or not they are valid. They appear to us at least to arise naturally and inevitably out of the lessons the past endeavors to teach us.

# 2

## THE NATURE OF
## JESUS' ACCOMPLISHMENT

❖❖❖❖❖❖ Jesus did not think and work in a vacuum. Nor was
he "a man from Mars" invading a totally foreign region with superhuman knowledge. In other words, he was a genuine human being.
He shared with all men the biological and psychological characteristics that distinguish man from animals and trees. No more than any
other man, however, was he simply man. Man is always German or
Japanese or American, white or brown or black, free or enslaved—and
there are no exceptions. To be man is by definition to be *a* man within
a specific historical and cultural context. It is to be born of woman to
a definite heritage and environment, and, soon or late, to die. The
cradle of Jesus was ancient Judaism. Within that historical and cultural framework he was born and within it he lived and died. Within
that context his individuality expressed itself in characteristically
Jewish ways. He transcended ancient Judaism, to be sure, as others
break free from a given setting, but he accomplished this effect as
a Jew among Jews. Everything about him was in this respect time-
caught: his presuppositions and his ideas, their forms of expression,
and the pattern and habits of his actions. His greatness consisted in

what he did as a native of Judaism. The universal and the timeless dimensions of Jesus were expressed in a particularistic setting and form.

Speaking theologically, the Incarnation was a real Incarnation. He was not an abstract Idea or a disembodied Spirit. He was an individual personality whose divine insights originated in a human mind and were embodied in the flesh of a human being. The inference is that, if we would understand Jesus realistically, we must interpret him with reference to his background.

We know enough about ancient Judaism to make this a reasonable possibility. One of the great advances in biblical studies in recent years has been increased information in this area. More than ever before we are equipped to set the career and thought of Jesus against a realistic backdrop, and thus to understand him better. There is danger in this procedure, to be sure, one that some interpreters of Jesus do not avoid. It is the hazard of so concentrating on the features Jesus has in common with his contemporaries as to be blinded to the unique and distinctive differences. This is not a built-in feature of the subject, however, but a failure in insight and proportion, which can be corrected. Jesus was not just like every other first century Jew because he was one of them. To think so is to make the same mistake as those who presume that Shakespeare, because he was an Elizabethan, must have been just like every other Elizabethan. A discriminating judgment will make it clear that the more discerningly we picture Jesus' setting, the more obvious becomes his remarkable individuality.

By way of illustration we appeal again to the example of Lincoln. Almost intuitively, when we read certain expressions of Lincoln, we sense the marvel of his superiority of character to that of others. Among other things, we sense his magnanimity toward his enemies or his ability to distinguish between primary and secondary objectives in the war. But only as we understand the currents of hatred and the other pressures against which he set his face during the war years can we profoundly appreciate his accomplishment. The uniqueness of this achievement becomes even more emphatic when we recall the aftermath of his death. A flood of vindictiveness was let loose upon the South that was contrary to his spirit and intentions, and that, had he lived, he would have opposed.

So it is with Jesus. If we would understand him with the percep-

tion of depth, and thus fully appreciate him, we must know his background. At least we must know enough to be intelligent in interpreting
him.

This book centers attention upon this necessity. It seeks to portray
Jesus' basic ideas in terms of their existence in Judaism and with particular attention to their nature as reactions to Judaism. Here we
consider the broader context in which his ideas were expressed. To
be specific, we concern ourselves with the nature of Jesus' originality
and the way in which he conceived of and expressed his sense of mission. We shall point out ways in which he was thoroughly and characteristically the Jew, other than in his basic ideas, and the manner
of his transcendence of his Jewishness.

## JESUS THE JEW

In developing this theme it is not required that we be exhaustive.
We shall content ourselves with indicating briefly the political and
economic setting of Jesus' life, and then point out a few ways in
which Jesus in his thought was characteristically Jewish. It is more
important to see how Jesus transcended this setting.

Jesus lived in an occupied country. Long before his birth the
Roman Eagle had spread its wings over the entire Mediterranean
area, its sharp beak having destroyed all opposition except on the
borders of the Empire. Palestine had succumbed in 63 B.C. Generally
speaking, Roman rule was beneficent and Roman policy in dealing
with the Jews was relatively liberal. The Jews were restive and resent-
ful, however, and many disturbances and much bloodshed marked
the period during which Jesus lived. When he was a boy a number of
rebellious Jews had been crucified at Sepphoris, about five miles north
of Nazareth. This was not an isolated instance. Thus Jesus must have
been familiar with the oppressive tactics of the Romans when they
were challenged.

The resentment against the Romans was watered by deep springs
of discontent, going back many years. Jesus inherited the memory of
his people of centuries of foreign occupation. Just prior to the Roman
conquest the Maccabees had gained for the Jews a brief period of
political as well as religious independence. Except for that, however,
the Jews had to look back beyond the Babylonian Exile in the sixth

century for any memory of political independence. Nostalgia recalled especially the reign of David long years before the Exile, and made it one important facet of nationalistic hopes for the future.

The agents employed by Rome to govern Palestine did not increase the popularity of the master race. Herod the Great (37–4 B.C.) was especially resented because of his Hellenistic sympathies and his cruelty, despite his efforts to placate the Jews by rebuilding the temple. His sons who followed him were no more successful in winning acclaim: Archelaus in Judea and Samaria, Antipas in Galilee and Peraea, and Philip in the northern regions. The procurators who replaced Archelaus in 6 B.C., of whom Pilate is best known to us, did not govern well and were constantly in hot water with their subjects. Taxation was especially exasperating to the Jews. Thus the publican, a subordinate tax collector, became the hated symbol of oppression.

Resentment against the Roman overlord took different forms. Whatever its form of expression, however, it was a staple of Jewish sentiment. The Sadducees were the least overt in opposition. Controlling the temple and the political offices, at the behest of Rome, they collaborated on the basis of expediency. The Pharisees were passive resisters, only on the rarest occasions taking up the sword. The Essenes retired to the desert to await God's direct intervention in the circumstances. The underground, later designated Zealots, worked assiduously to force God's hand by stirring up active revolt. Some forty years after the death of Jesus they succeeded, except that God's hand came down upon them in a manner quite contrary to their expectations. The results were futile and disastrous. Jerusalem was destroyed and the temple was forever erased as the focal point of Judaism. The religious life of Judaism from that time on centered in the synagogues. Even before A.D. 70, when Jerusalem fell, the synagogue had fastened itself upon the hearts of the Jews.

To all intents and purposes Jesus took no active part in politics, and his attitude cannot be exactly equated with any of these points of view. If he resented Roman occupation, he did not say so. On one occasion he implied that within its own sphere of operation Roman taxation had its rights. He also made tax collectors his companions. He was most certainly neither Sadducee nor Essene nor Zealot. If we must classify him, he was more Pharisee in this respect than any other. Yet he was not a typical Pharisee. In this respect, as in most others, he cannot be adequately classified. He was completely himself. This independence of mind with regard to politics actually set him off from every group in his environment, and was one contributing cause of his crucifixion.

Economically speaking, Jesus apparently belonged among the numerous artisans. There was a great variety of trades. In that category Jesus was thus neither rich, like the Sadducees with their landed estates, nor poverty-stricken like the few slaves and the more numerous tenant farmers. Familiar though he was with agricultural procedures, he was not one of the many farmers who cultivated their fields and vineyards. Although he was aware of the active life of trade that characterized his region, he was not a merchant. Living in a small town, distinguished perhaps by its guild of carpenters and masons, he learned his father's trade and practiced it until his public ministry began.

Like most Pharisees, then, he was a plebian rather than an aristocrat. His sympathies, however, were with those who were called "the people of the land" (*'am ha-ares*). Originally this term distinguished the common people from the nobility and the priesthood, later, the untutored from serious students of the Law. Probably it had in Jesus' day both an economic and a religious connotation. If not all in this classification were "poor" in this world's goods, many surely were. The more important distinction was of a religious character. Set over against "the people of the land" were "the associates" (*haberim*), who banded together for stricter observance of the levitical precepts. They looked down upon the former because of their indifference to or carelessness about ritualistic scruples. The moral tenor of the lives of "the people of the land" might be very high, inspired by a warm and vigorous religion of the heart, even though many of them were probably no more serious about religion than many nominal Christians today. When they were of a serious mind in this matter, their outlook was nonlegalistic. Jesus' affinity for these "sinners" is one of the prominent marks of his attitude. It too became a contributing cause of his crucifixion at the hands of the orthodox.

Turning to the question of Jesus' Jewishness in specifically religious terms, we are reminded that all life was viewed religiously by the Jew. However, certain features of Jewish life may be designated as narrowly religious. At this point we shall review certain of these features to the extent that they help us to envisage clearly the Jewishness of Jesus. To describe Jewish habits of thought and practice is to picture Jesus himself in most respects.

The first feature to be treated is the nature of Jewish thought on religious matters. There was no systematic theological thinking in the modern sense of the term. One looks in vain among the writings of ancient Jews for a logical and coherent treatment of theological topics like that in outstanding modern books. There is nothing to correspond to R. Bultmann's *Theology of the New Testament*. There is not even a simplified treatment like A. M. Hunter's *Introducing New Testament Theology*, a very useful guide for the thoughtful layman. There was of course a basic set of propositions. Judaism in that sense had a creed. There was also a great deal of speculation in the schools on religious and theological issues. There was consistency of a sort with regard to essential convictions, even though there was also much difference of opinion with regard to their implications and meanings.

In three respects at least, however, Jewish religious thought differed from "systematic theology" as defined by a modern point of view. First, it was thoroughly practical in its bearing and interest. What mattered was the practice of religion in daily life, not coherence of thought. The elaboration or the revision of ideas was important only as it contributed to that end. Rethinking of ideas was itself inspired by some practical contingency in the first place. In other words, the relevance of ideas to current needs was uppermost in the minds of the Jews. How did religion apply to daily life? That is what mattered. Expressed more precisely, the purpose and the intent of theological thinking were the adequate application of time-honored truths to immediate dilemmas. Thus Judaism was characterized as a religion of practice rather than of speculation.

In the second place, theological thought was more intuitive than logical or "scientific." A subject was not thought through consistently from basic premises to a conclusion that followed inevitably from a survey of the relevant evidence. Unlike the Greeks, the Hebrews made no contribution to scientific thought. They were not interested in natural phenomena from that point of view, nor did they think "scientifically." Because of this, contradictory or paradoxical ideas might be held at the same time. T. E. Lawrence observed this phenomenon among modern Semites. His words must be accepted advisedly as a fully accurate description of Jewish thinking in Jesus' day, but with that reservation in mind they are not entirely inappropriate. He writes:

They inhabited superlatives by choice. Sometimes inconsistencies seemed to possess them at once in joint sway; but they never compromised; they pursued the logic of several incompatible opinions to absurd ends, without perceiving the incongruity.

A better analogy is provided by the words of E. Stanley Jones, commenting upon the observation of Acharya Kripalani that Gandhi "is more right when he is wrong than we are when we are right":

His spirit and magnificent intention carried him past mental detours and brought him almost unerringly to his goal. His spirit was so great that it could absorb mental limitations and make something great even out of them. . . . He thought clearly because his intentions were simple and clear. He was not intellectually brilliant, but he was so fundamentally straight that his moral intentions carried him almost by intuition to right conclusions.

Obviously this indicates Hebrew thought at its best, in the great prophets and predominantly in Jesus. It does not characterize the mood of legalism in Jesus' time. Still, the distinction between an intuitive and a rationalistic approach to ideas stands as significant in understanding the Jewish mind.

In the third place, with direct reference to the thought of the scribes, there was no effort to coordinate interpretations of the Law in a systematic manner. The individual scribe might be more or less consistent in certain respects. Thus we can distinguish the basic spirit and its consequences in specific interpretations of Hillel from Shammai, two famous scribes in ancient Judaism. When we turn to the Jewish tradition as it became fixed in writing, however, we can observe its uncoordinated nature. This tradition reposes in the Mishna and the two versions (Palestinian and Babylonian) of the Talmud, which came into being at the end of the second century and later.

The Mishna and the Talmuds contain successive interpretations of many scribes over many years. These interpretations correspond to the court decisions in our country designed to clarify the meaning of the basic Constitution with reference to specific issues as they arise.

They concern litigation and jurisprudence, the object being to bring the ancient Law up to date or to apply the general principle to specific questions. A large part of this deals with regulations for the observance of the Sabbath. How to keep that day holy, especially with respect to what was and what was not considered to be work, aroused extensive discussion. The various judgments of many scribes did not always agree. They might even be contradictory.

In codifying this material the rabbis who were responsible for the Mishna and the Talmuds did not see fit to coordinate or to systematize the interpretations. Contradictory interpretations simply are recorded side by side. The most Jewish of our Gospels, that according to Matthew, illustrates this habit of mind. On one occasion Jesus is reported as instructing his disciples to confine their missionary activity to Jews, avoiding Gentiles, but at the end the resurrected Jesus sends them into all the world. The two views simply stand by themselves without any attempt to reconcile them. So it is with our records of Jewish legalistic interpretation.

The Mishna and the Talmuds of course contain much material that is later than the time of Jesus, and perhaps what we are saying about the Jewish mentality that is illustrated by it represents more the habits of a later period than that in which Jesus lived. It is difficult to distinguish within this material between the different periods, however, and that itself suggests that the habit of mind we are portraying was characteristic of Jewish thinking in every period.

When we attempt to place Jesus within this context, it is obvious that he was more the prophet than the scribe. The point is valid, however, that as such he was thoroughly the Jew as against the Greek. His teaching was unsystematic and occasional. Furthermore, it was "always a prelude to action." It was "always directed toward practical ends affecting the relationship between God and man." It was poetical and graphic rather than rationalistic and abstract. That is, like his contemporaries—or like the best of his race—he belonged to the sphere of religion rather than of (systematic) theology, let alone that of science.

Certain additional features of ancient Jewish thought and practice are so obviously characteristic of Jesus that we need not labor the point unduly. As we proceed in a moment to analyze something of the creative way in which Jesus reacted to his heritage and his environment, we shall be aware at all times of the groundwork of Judaism on which he stood. Thus a few summary sentences will suffice for our purpose in addition to what has already been said.

It is reasonable to assume that Jesus' education and training followed that of the prevailing customs. This meant that he received instruction in the home and eventually in the synagogue (school as well as church). Before he could fully understand what was involved he would have learned an attitude of prayer, and also been impressed with many symbolic actions on the part of his parents. Journeys to the Passover and other national festivals in Jerusalem would have impressed upon him the religious meaning of Israel's history and destiny. In synagogue school and worship he would have learned the scriptures of his people. His teaching shows him immersed in the thought and phraseology of his scriptures. His speech is rich and overflowing with literary allusions (a vineyard, and so on), historical allusions (David, Solomon), and direct quotations (the Great Commandment). As we shall see, his ideas are grounded in the Old Testament. His forms of speech, notably Hebrew poetical parallelism and the parable, were those common to Jewish prophets and teachers. In these and many other ways he fits into the world of first century Judaism as a native son of a great heritage.

## JESUS THE CREATIVE JEW

When we grant all this, however, we have only begun to tell his story. It is the same with him as with Paul. We take note of Paul's threefold heritage—Hebrew, Greek, and Roman—and recognize its significance, but what is most important about Paul is the way in which he reacted to it. Jesus was a first century Jew, but he was so creative and so original within that context as to impress himself upon mankind in an unprecedented manner. He has no rivals among the great of his own race, including Moses, nor is he seriously challenged by any other member of the human race. This is an amazing thing.

When we seek within the Gospels the explanation of this fact we do not find a complete answer. There are factors involved that are hidden from human analysis and understanding. God alone knows the complete answer. This of course is true of any person, despite advances in psychology and psychoanalysis. Every individual is a mysterious entity that defies complete analysis. Thus we should not be deterred from trying to understand as much as we can of the sources of Jesus' uniqueness. A study of the Gospels with this in mind does yield valid results. There are marks of individuality, singularity, uniqueness, genius that point in the direction of as much of an explanation as it is historically possible to attain. The record, in every level of tradition, is completely consistent. There is a sovereign independence about Jesus that cannot be explained by or contained within the limitations of any category of Judaism. He is thoroughly like his compatriots in every basic respect, yet he is also so unlike any one of them in terms of his creativity that he becomes a universal figure. He transcends that of which he is thoroughly a part. There is a new wine in his individuality that old forms can neither explain nor contain.

Properly to estimate this fact about Jesus requires us to ask the right questions about its nature. The question of Jesus' originality has too often been clouded by false assumptions as to the meaning of originality. It has been assumed, for instance, that Jesus was not original because Jewish sayings can be found to parallel practically all of his utterances. But this is a false idea of originality. If Jesus were lacking in originality on that basis, he would never have been heard of beyond his own day. The place to begin is with that presupposition. He must have done something extremely creative with the raw materials he shared with his people to produce the unprecedented effect that history records. When we permit this presupposition to prepare our minds to ask the right questions, it is not difficult to ascertain the factors relevant to their answers.

The originality of Jesus was not in kind like that of the nuclear physicists who discovered the neutron and split the atom. It did not, as it were, "create" something entirely new. It is rather the type that uses well-worn stones from an old building in order to erect a new structure. It worked with age-old ideas, which were not the sole possession of the Jews, to the end of new perspectives. It was like the genius of a Shakespeare. His plays cannot be confused with those of any other playwright. They are uniquely Shakespeare and no other. Yet they express ideas the author did not create, and they reveal traces of literary dependence upon earlier writers. The essence of this type of originality is well expressed in these words: "Everything depends upon the particular way ideas are conceived, the way in which their force is felt, the way they are related to one another in some kind of personal synthesis, and the way in which they are expressed." With reference to Lincoln, Lord Charnwood both corroborates and supplements this definition. He wrote:

When [the war] was over it seemed to the people that he had all along been thinking their real thoughts for them; but they knew that this was because he had fearlessly thought for himself. . . . This most unrelenting enemy to the project of the Confederacy was the one man who had quite purged his heart and mind from hatred or even anger towards his fellow-countrymen of the South. That fact came to be seen in the South too, and generations in America are likely to remember it when all other features of his statecraft have grown indistinct.

A modern historian supports this latter idea when he says that our greatest legacy from the past is, along with that of Washington, the character of Lincoln. This adds to the first definition quoted above the dimension of character. An aspect of genius in this area concerns what a man is as well as the way he thinks.

We may go one step further. The essential ingredients of a definition of originality adequate to the understanding of Jesus have been set down. However, we wish to penetrate a little deeper, bringing out other facets of this kind of originality. To that end we quote Walter Lippmann's estimate of what he calls the genius of General Charles de Gaulle, a genius shared in this generation only with Winston Churchill. We are not concerned with the accuracy of Lippmann's evaluation of De Gaulle. We recognize also that De Gaulle operates in a sphere that was not that of Jesus' work. At the same time we see in the characteristics that are depicted true marks of genius in any realm. This is what Lippmann says:

His genius consists in the capacity to see beneath the surface of events, to see through the obvious and stereotyped appearance of events to the significant realities, to the obscured facts and forces which will prevail. This gift, which is more than leadership as such, is second sight into the nature of history. It brings with it the gift of prophesying what is going to happen because to the seeing eye it is already there. The ability to see truly the significant reality carries with it the ability to convey what his vision brings him.

This suggests much about the nature of the originality and the genius of Jesus, despite the differences between De Gaulle and him. It is amazing how directly applicable it is to Jesus' mind and achievement.

Applying these various expressions explicitly to Jesus, there are three facets of them to be distinguished. There is first the gift of expression, what Lippmann calls "the ability to convey what his vision brings forth." There is, in the second place, everything that characterizes the ability of the mind to ascertain meanings in things. Lippmann's definition as a whole is applicable, as well as the references to the way in which ideas are conceived, their force felt, and their relationship to one another in a personal synthesis created. The independence of a Lincoln also belongs under this heading. In the third place, there is the fundamental aspect of the character of a man inspired by an intense and realistic relationship to God, as in the quotation of Lord Charnwood.

Each of these facets of the subject can be illustrated fully from the Gospels. What we intend to do here, however, is dictated by the organization of the book. The second and the third of these elements will appear in the development of the theme in subsequent chapters. This applies particularly to the second one. It becomes obvious that Jesus gave a new center of interest and a new emphasis to old ideas through the way in which he modified them and related them to one another. We shall leave until later pages the illustrations of this evident fact. They will emerge naturally by inference from the treatment of the subject. The third element requires a short exposition at this point, which will be undertaken. It is the first element, however, that will be more fully expounded in this chapter because it will not appear, except incidentally, at any later point.

We consider then the character of Jesus with reference to the question of his originality. The teaching of Jesus was as much a life as a set of ideas. As it has been said, Jesus' ideas "have the penetrating warmth of intense personal experience and not a chill abstraction generally characteristic of their presentation in more philosophical connections." He experienced and he lived what he taught. The decisions he called his disciples to make were decisions he himself had already made. The qualities of character he held up as being God's will were those he himself had achieved. Greatness has been defined as "an extraordinary capacity for achievement." This includes a Napoleon as well as a Pasteur. The greatness of Jesus, as judged by this criterion, contains the element of a beneficent achievement growing out of the quality of his life. That is, he was "great as a man." In the sum total of the qualities that merge within a person to produce his character, Jesus is unsurpassed. The two fundamental ingredients of that character are obedience and self-giving love.

There are those who have seen fit to challenge the character of Jesus on one point, that of his love of enemies. It is claimed that his treatment of the scribes and Pharisees does not exemplify that which he taught. This is to misunderstand the nature of love. It is not sentimentality. Love can be as critical and as stern as the intelligent parent in disciplining the child. The criterion lies in the area of motivation and method. Jesus never wished his enemies harm. He protested against their ideas and practices, but he also wept over their blindness, and he went to the cross as much for their sake as for that of his friends. The legacy of his character, like that of Lincoln, is central in the explanation of his originality and his genius.

Jesus' awareness of God as alive and active, experienced and voiced with unusual intensity, undergirds as it coheres with this aspect of his person. He had a unique sense of the reality of God and of God's expression of himself in and through him. So intense was this that Jesus assumed the prerogative of standing in the place of God in pronouncing judgment upon evil and offering forgiveness to repentant sinners. This is the historical root of the doctrine of the Incarnation, if by that we mean that "the humanity of Jesus of Nazareth was completely united with God, and . . . everything he did and said as man was at the same time the work and activity of God." We should distinguish this attitude, however, from that of the mystic who feels that he is becoming absorbed in God. Jesus does not use such language of himself. He simply makes the assertion, in life as in words, that the God about whom he teaches is the God whom he experiences in worship and whom he is conscious of serving without reservations. To the extent that he embodies God's will and his power, it is as instrument and not as equal in an ultimate sense. He sees God because he is "pure in heart." This links his character with his religious experience. The one was of ultimate dimensions because the other was so profound and so true.

To speak of Jesus as "sinless" in these respects is to make an assertion that cannot be demonstrated. We do not know whether or not Jesus was ever disobedient to God. Luke says that he grew not only in stature but also "in favor with God." Growth in any realistic sense means learning from mistakes. It is, however, an academic question. That Jesus achieved a character of unequaled splendor is unquestionable. It is the testimony of the record and of his impact upon mankind. That is all we need to know about it.

We consider now, in more detail, Jesus' capacity in the area of expression. It is the other facet of his originality that has previously been designated. We cannot, strictly speaking, describe this as "literary form," since he was not a writer. Granting that, we can appreciate the estimate of his ability in the following words: "The words and discourses of Jesus . . . bear comparison with the most finished products of the human mind, and ought to be ranked among the masterpieces of world literature." Let us distinguish several aspects of this genius in expression.

Speaking comprehensively, there was nothing of the platitude in Jesus' words. There were vitality and freshness of form as well as of content, even though the specific forms were those common to Jewish prophets and teachers. With this in mind we recall the situation in a class in English. The teacher was trying to help a pupil avoid the use of cliché or stereotyped expression that had lost its cutting edge through overusage. The following poem was the result:

### B. C. (Before Cliché)

#### Morning

I watched a fluffy cloud drift by
Across the boundless blue of sky
And saw the sun's rays, molten gold,
Upon the dewy earth unfold.

#### Evening

I felt my fettered soul uplift
Before the rosy sunset drift
And in the hazy blue afar
I saw the gleaming evening star.

### A. D. (After Discovering—'em)

#### Morning
I saw the sun with battered face
Trying to warm the human race;
I watched a sodden cloud limp by
Like some discouraged custard pie.

#### Evening
The sleepy sun in flannels red
Went yawning to its Western bed;
I saw one shivering small star
No brighter than our dishpans are.

Jesus probably never heard of cliché, but he did know how to avoid —'em! He used well-worn words and images, but he put them together creatively.

Being more concrete, we note first his use of imagery and picture-language. He gives no abstract or theoretical definitions. Everything is made graphic and concrete, even when it is symbolical. His dominant theme, the kingdom (reign) of God, is defined only by means of comparison with a mustard seed or leaven or some human situation. His images, found on every page of the Gospels, are drawn from all walks of life: wineskins hanging in the house, a farmer sowing his seed and reaping the harvest, a shepherd tending his sheep, a widow seeking justice from a reluctant judge, flowers in a field, birds in the sky or in the trees, and so forth. The capacity for the picturesque comes to its apex in the parable form. In an imaginative picture taken from real life, Jesus drives home his ideas about God and human relations: a lost son returning home, a lost sheep, children playing at weddings and funerals, a Pharisee and a publican praying in the temple, a man robbed on the barren Jericho road, and so forth. His use of conscious exaggeration (hyberbole) constitutes a "gigantesque" feature of his way of saying things, so as to startle and awaken his listeners. A camel labors to squeeze through a needle's eye; a man with a plank in his eye tries vainly to remove the speck from the eye of another; a huge millstone is tied about the neck of one insensitive to his weaker brethren and is hurled into the sea; and a mountain is uprooted and thrown into the waters. Jesus' language is replete with such graphic expressions. In fact this is his language.

Certain other aspects of Jesus' "literary" ability involve more than a form of expression. His ability to concentrate upon what is essential, along with a sense of reality, affects his manner of speech. This is seen in the way in which the form of his utterance is perfectly adapted to its content. This manifests a simplicity and a directness that shun artificial striving for effect and hair-splitting definitions, and employ the most living and simple expression. The ultimate test of good form is that, without being noticed as such, it serves as a perfect instrument for creative expression. When the thought or the idea comes home forcefully to the mind and heart, then one can sense that it is skillfully done, whether it be a play or a sermon or a single saying. Jesus' parables perfectly represent this quality of expression. The Parable of the Prodigal Son, for example, is skillfully framed, with no unnecessary or distracting appendages, everything contributing to its one point. When one reads it with a responsive spirit, he is moved by the extravagance of God's forgiving mercy, and he resents the contrasting reaction of the older brother. The effect is due to the form as well as to the content. This capacity of Jesus is abundantly evident in the Gospels.

In the same category is Jesus' instinctive ability in debate to cut through all non-essentials and place his finger upon the heart of the subject under discussion. His paradoxes illustrate this, such as those about paying taxes to Caesar and losing life to find it. It is evident especially in Jesus' polemical utterances. With regard to Sabbath violation, Jesus stymies his opponents with the only question that matters, whether a man is as important as an animal. Facing a challenge to his authority, he puts his questioners on the defensive by asking whether the authority of John the Baptist was of human or divine origin.

This but scratches the surface of Jesus' capacity to express himself. It is but one of the facets of his originality, joined in synthesis with his character and his genius in thought. Enough has been said to indicate its nature and meaning in a preliminary manner, as we leave until later pages its manifestation in other ways.

## JESUS' SENSE OF AUTHORITY

The question of the nature of Jesus' accomplishment involves more than the question of his originality along the lines on which we have been discussing it. It leads directly into the area of his sense of authority. That he acted with a sovereign independence, implying an unprecedented authority, hardly needs to be demonstrated to any reader of the Gospels. He implied in the Parable of the Vineyard that he had come to his people at God's behest as the culminating representative of the divine will and that judgment was definitely determined by the way in which he was received. His authority, he was convinced, was "from heaven." The people recognized the unusual stance he assumed when they said that it was "with authority" (freedom of action) that he taught and exorcized demons. His crucifixion is negative testimony to the powerful impact he made upon his contemporaries. It joins with many data of both a positive and a negative kind to reinforce the impressions of his authoritative bearing that have just been indicated.

The specific question with which we are concerned at this point is that of how we are to understand the mind of Jesus within the context of his Jewish orientation. Within his mind and experience what were the springs of his unusual sense of authority? How did he picture himself with reference to his mission, his vocation? This involves us immediately in titles and offices, even though the subject is much more inclusive.

If it is Jesus' immediate environment against which we seek to picture him, there are many titles that are automatically eliminated. The term "genius" is a modern, not an ancient, term. The phrases of the Nicene Creed were outside his frame of reference. He would have been baffled by the controversy over two terms differing only in one letter: *homoousios* ("of one essence with the Father") and *homoiousios* ("like the Father"). "Word" or "Logos" as employed in John's Gospel belonged to a type of thought not native to him. Even "Lord" would not have appealed to such a monotheist as he was, since it was a standard term for God. If he used it of himself, it could only have been as "Master."

The only available titles were those common to Jewish thought: Rabbi or Teacher, Prophet, Messiah, Servant. Within the scope of messianic ideas there were Son of David, Son of man, Son of God. If we are to explain Jesus' sense of authority in terms of a title, we must confine ourselves to these.

The striking fact about the Gospels is that no title really suits him.

In this respect, as in every other, he was extremely unconventional and completely himself. From whatever vantage point we view him, he stands alone, and we are unable to explain him by means of any category within his setting. He was no party man. He was neither Sadducee, Pharisee, Essene, nor Zealot. He was a Galilean instead of a Judean, which accounts for some things about him but does not really explain him. The same can be said for the fact that he was a Palestinian instead of a Hellenistic Jew. These are the accidents of his life, important so far as they go, but not significant when we seek to understand his sense of authority. The same is true of traditional titles. If he employed any single one of them, or several in combination, he so transformed them as to make them unrecognizable by his contemporaries. He was an independent thinker in this area as elsewhere.

We must examine the question more closely, however, and to that end we suggest three headings. First, we consider the problem of titles assigned to him in the Gospels. Second, we note his disinclination to be specific about the question of his vocation as compared with his heavy emphasis upon God and his purposes. Third, on that basis we ask about the fundamental ingredients of Jesus' sense of authority irrespective of titles.

With regard to the titles Jesus employs or which are applied to him, the Gospels give us a confused picture. The most consistent note is that Jesus called himself Son of man. This would mean that Jesus thought of himself as the messiah of Jewish expectations. It would mean in addition that he made a choice between the two dominant conceptions of the messiah prevalent in his day, preferring the conception of a preexistent heavenly man to that of a nationalistic Davidic figure. Since the two conceptions overlapped to a certain extent, he might have merged them in his thought. If we assume that Jesus so designated himself, we are confronted with some very perplexing problems. There is little question that he repudiated a narrow and exclusive nationalism in all its forms. That sent the idea of Davidic messiahship out the window, except in a symbolical sense. The Gospels confirm this unequivocally. With regard to the Son of man title, however, the case is quite different. Certain sayings of Jesus are in line with the expectation of the Son of man at the Last Day, but how could Jesus have thought that he was this preexistent

figure whose appearance was to be wholly in the future? Other sayings link Jesus as Son of man with his suffering and death, and there
was no precedent for that. The Son of man was a conquering messiah,
not a defeated one. He would come gloriously on the clouds of
heaven, not be raised up on a cross. His coming would be the defeat
of God's enemies, not their triumph over God's agent. These and
related problems revolve around the attempt to understand Jesus'
mind in terms of Son of man messiahship.

The same perplexing situation exists when we attempt to consider the title Son of God as more appropriate to him, let alone
"Lord" or "Servant" or "Word." This is an area in which scholarly opinion has solved nothing. Judgments fluctuate hither and yon,
always in the realm of probabilities and possibilities, but with no
conclusive solution. Nor can it be otherwise, since the Gospels will
always be just as ambiguous as they now are.

It is very easy to conclude that the reason for this confusion in the
records is due to Jesus himself. He did not define his sense of mission
in unequivocal terms or give instruction about his vocation in this
way. That is, his treatment of this issue was like that of his teaching
about the kingdom (reign) of God. He gave no formal definition.
Others would say that he believed himself to be messiah, but that
his transformation of its meaning made it unintelligible to his contemporaries. In order to prevent misunderstanding he kept it secret,
but others guessed his secret and proclaimed him messiah. But this
aspect of the records looks more like a theory of Mark imposed upon
the data than Jesus' own thought. Others vary this by saying that he
never claimed to be messiah but that he acted like messiah. His astounding claims of authority in regard to the Sabbath and other
Jewish regulations and in dealing with demon-possessed people were
like those of the expected messiah at the End. Thus he acted mes-
sianically even if he did not claim the title.

There are still other theories. All that they indicate is the confusion of scholarship and the futility of thinking that the question
can ever be settled on this level. There is a better way. It is to ascertain
from his teachings and actions the nature of his authority, however
we may label it. In that way we come close to his mind in the matter.
We come as close to it as the records will permit, and there need be
no uncertainty in that respect about some very important things.

Furthermore, we have to do this anyway even when we concentrate upon any given title. As any title stands it is a neutral quantity. It has a traditional meaning, but its meaning for Jesus is something else. The latter can only be determined by analyzing what he thought about the nature of his authority. Having decided that, and only then, can we interpret what he might have meant by Son of man, Son of God, or any other title. When we begin a discussion of this kind with the titles themselves, we pick up the wrong end of the stick.

Leaving the titles aside for the moment, we turn to consider the second facet of our subject. This consists of Jesus' apparent disinclination to discuss the question of his mission or of his status before God, because he was completely concentrated upon God and his purposes for himself. The records are not entirely consistent on this point either, but the clouds are not so thick as in the area of titles.

The point of view assumed here is implied by way of analogy in words of Mark Van Doren under the title of "The Good Teacher." In the course of an exposition of the teacher's responsibility to his pupils, he writes:

The teacher's responsibility to his subject is so serious a thing that it of course precludes anything like a parade of personality for its own sake. The good teacher is not trying to be a personality; he is trying to be a person who understands his subject and sinks himself into it. If he could he would disappear there altogether.

Jesus' subject was God, not himself. He submerged himself so completely in God and his purposes, with the teacher's eagerness to transmit his subject to his pupils, that he gave relatively little attention to himself as such. If he did think about his vocational ideal or his sense of mission in more specific terms, it was only that he might the better portray and transmit his subject.

That this was Jesus' feeling about himself and his mission finds sustaining evidence in the Gospels. It is the burden of the Lord's Prayer, the ideal pattern from his lips. Everything in the prayer concerns God: his fatherly nature, his holiness, his reign, his demands upon men, his power to forgive and to sustain life. The kingdom about which Jesus focuses his message is the reign of *God.* Gethsemane brings the crisis in Jesus' life to its climax. The problem is not what Jesus shall call himself, but what he shall do. It is not a question of status, but of a task to be completed. And the task about which the crucial problem of suffering centers is one assigned by God. This is Jesus' emphasis throughout. He even directs attention away from himself, from his goodness, toward God, in rebuking the young man who called him "Good master." "No one is good but God alone," he replied. God mattered, he did not. As compared with the necessity of fulfilling God's will for him even his life was cheap. This is something quite different from keeping his alleged messiahship a secret. It is a refusal to take himself that seriously with respect to the glory and the power of God.

At the same time there are sayings of Jesus that reveal him as taking very seriously the idea that God had granted him an authority not given to others. Not only in explicit statements but also in the implications of his teaching and work this becomes evident. We shall cite typical examples rather than attempt to be exhaustive. "All things have been delivered to me by my Father," he says, and he amplifies the thought along the lines of the emphasis in John's Gospel. In that Gospel Jesus is revealer of God and mediator of his salvation in an exclusive sense. The phraseology, even the way of conceiving Jesus' status, that characterize John's Gospel are not characteristic of the first three Gospels. However, the basic assumption is the same. He has come to seek and save the lost, and he has been sent by God for that purpose. A series of events indicates by implication Jesus' high vocational sense. These events include the Baptism, the Temptation, the Caesarea Philippi scene and the Transfiguration, the Triumphal Entry, the Anointing, the Cleansing of the Temple, and the Last Supper. There is reason to believe that in this type of report the reactions of the early Christians have been prominently expressed. The interpretative element is strong. They undoubtedly contain a core that is reliable, and some of the interpretation is consistent with less-interpreted sayings of Jesus. It is better, however, to look elsewhere for clues to Jesus' essential mind.

There are indications that Jesus felt that the decision for God that he called upon men to make was at the same time a decision regarding himself. The Parable of the Houses implies that reception of his teaching is the criterion of judgment. Other sayings are even more explicit. To acknowledge him on earth is to guarantee acknowledgment by him before God in the judgment. The same sentiment is expressed when Jesus weeps over Jerusalem and laments its failure to receive him. The Parable of the Wicked Husbandmen, previously cited, carries the same note.

We may add the implications of his polemical teaching. In controversy with the Jewish leaders he assumed a sovereign authority even to challenge the sacred Law of Judaism. New ideas require new forms of expression, just as new wine must be poured into new wineskins. Jesus not only challenged the personal failures of the leaders; he also attacked the institution of the Sabbath. Rather, he attacked current interpretations of how it should be observed. He went against much Oral Tradition in this and other respects, and even appeared to belittle the written Law itself in certain ways. This was, from the scribal point of view, to set himself above Moses. It was in fact to set himself above God, since scribal theory taught that the Law was God's revelation of his will. In parables like that of the Prodigal Son we sense Jesus' assumption of an authority quite different in kind from that of the scribes. The Parable of the Prodigal was not an abstract lesson about God's forgiving grace. It was directed against the leaders whose attitude was that of the older brother in the parable. As Jesus set himself against that attitude, he assumed the right to speak for God, actually to stand in God's place. His sovereign independence presupposed a very high sense of authority.

There are a few more explicit sayings that imply much about Jesus' thought of his own status. He equates the authority of John the Baptist with his own. It too is "from heaven," from God. John stands on the threshold of the new era that is being introduced with Jesus. As such he is more than a prophet, a very high estimate indeed of his status. Yet Jesus is far superior. There is something in Jesus that he views as greater than Jonah, greater than Solomon, greater even than the temple. His disciples are favored above all men to witness what God is bringing to pass in and through him. The call and commission of the disciples simply reemphasizes this conviction that he stands before his generation with a commission of his own from God that has no counterpart in the past or the present.

With all this in mind we cannot reasonably believe that Jesus did not give serious thought to his vocation and mission. His authoritative bearing is obvious. He claimed much for himself. At the same time there is no reason to interpret this high vocational sense out-

side the framework of his concentration upon God and his purposes.
That is, "the subject" of the teacher was predominant, not the
teacher himself. It was only that he might fulfill God's purposes for
mankind that he assumed such authority. If it were not God-given
and God-directed, it would be meaningless.

The resolution of the ultimate question with regard to Jesus' mind
in this area of thought leads us to consider material relevant to the
third division of the topic. Granting Jesus' consciousness of a unique
authority, what was its nature? This involves a comparison between
Jesus and scribe, but more especially between Jesus and prophet. It
culminates in the question as to whether we can define his authority as anything less, in Jewish terms, than that of messiah. Central to
this problem is the question of how Jesus viewed his suffering and
crucifixion.

Jesus said that John the Baptist was a prophet, but "more than a
prophet." He could have said the same thing about himself. He moved
in the prophetic mold in contrast to that of the rabbi or scribe. Rather,
he was a prophetic rabbi or teacher. He was a teacher. The records
are emphatic on that point, both explicitly and implicitly. He is called
a rabbi or teacher more than anything else, and he obviously taught.
He is also assumed to be a prophet, like his ancient forebears Amos,
Hosea, Isaiah, Jeremiah, and others. Occasionally, as at Nazareth, he
speaks of himself as a prophet. The point of this is the contrast between his bearing, and his method of dealing with issues, and that
of the Jewish lawyers and interpreters of the Law, the scribes. Jesus
assumed a direct and immediate knowledge of God that was completely foreign to the assumptions of the scribes. Theoretically both
Jesus and scribe believed in the sacredness of God's revelation of his
will in the scriptures. Actually, Jesus assumed that God spoke much
more directly to him within his mind and heart and conscience. The
people were astonished at this independence of the scriptures and of
the traditions that set Jesus off in such sharp contrast to the usual
scribal procedure of appealing to precedents. There was an astonish-
ing sovereignty about the way in which Jesus handled issues of religious thought and practice. There were also an aggressiveness about
Jesus and a radical seriousness about his challenge that differentiated
him from the scribes.

The primary question is the extent to which we can classify Jesus as a prophet. His bearing was prophetic. His sense of inner authority was that of the prophet. As the prophet considered himself a forth-teller of God's revealed will within his heart, so Jesus introduced certain teachings with an emphatic "I say to you." This corresponded to the prophetic "Thus says the Lord." There are other similarities. At a later point we shall have occasion to see the way in which Jesus was more prophetic than apocalyptic in his views about the future triumph of God's reign. Granting Jesus' essentially prophetic spirit in contrast to that of the scribe, the fact remains that in some ways he was "more than a prophet." In what ways? That is the question of greatest importance.

In at least five ways a distinction may be drawn between Jesus and the classical prophet. He made more of an appeal to man's reason and common sense than the prophet usually did. He combined something of the approach of the wise man, reflected in Proverbs, with that of the prophet. The latter was dogmatic. He was not opening a subject to discussion, but proclaiming a fact that man must take or leave. He spoke with God's voice, and it was not to be questioned. Jesus acted in that way too, most of the time, in fact. Yet he qualified that approach when he asked men to think about their anxiety: "Which of you by being anxious can add one cubit to his span of life?" He followed the same method in controversy over the healing of a paralytic and over healing on the Sabbath. These questions appear often to be more rhetorical than real, but they do indicate an appeal to man's reason.

Jesus considered the individual more than the prophet did. The latter voiced his message to the nation, the group. Jesus did likewise, although it is the leaders whom he addresses most frequently. On the whole, however, Jesus carried to its ultimate expression the individualism that had begun to be developed in Jewish thought during his time. His statements about rich men illustrate this. He said that it was more difficult for a rich man to enter the kingdom than for a camel to go through the eye of a needle. This is not a criticism of the social consequences of the rich man's self-interest, except by implication. Jesus is not thinking about the poor who needed a more equitable distribution of the national income. He is thinking about the fate of the rich man. He may well have in mind the rich young man who has just turned away from his offer of salvation because he could not dispossess himself of his privileges. The prophets condemned individual rulers, but their message of doom was directed largely at the group. It is Israel that is under judgment. For Jesus it is, on the whole, the individual.

The most striking difference between the classical prophet and Jesus concerns their respective views of time in relation to the fulfillment of God's purposes. The prophet arose in a crisis to pronounce God's judgment upon his People. He viewed that judgment as an event within history. Israel would suffer as a nation, but its history would not end. A new day could come if the People repented. Jesus, on the other hand, appeared to be convinced that an utterly new age was dawning with his ministry. The reign of God was not only coming at a future date, probably in the near future; in some sense it was present. It was dawning in his message and work. John the Baptist was in that sense his forerunner. This accounts for Jesus' estimate of the Baptist as "more than a prophet." He was the herald of the new age, the advance sign. Jesus was the full sign. In this respect he too was "more than a prophet."

Jesus called for an allegiance to himself that was not typical of the prophet. The prophet directed attention to his message rather than to himself, while Jesus felt that his message was embodied in his person. This has already been pointed out. Combined with it was Jesus' startling suggestion that, in a certain respect, he stood in God's place. He passed judgment and forgave sins for God. No prophet ever claimed so much as this.

Finally, Jesus gathered about him a group of intimate disciples to be with him and to assist him in spreading his message. Only by implication did he constitute this group as the nucleus of a future church, but the relationship between Jesus and them is without parallel among the ancient prophets. It is the status that Jesus assumed for himself, as just stated, that actually made the relationship between himself and his disciples unique. If the prophets had disciples, their relationship was quite different from that of Jesus' disciples to Jesus.

All this would appear to suggest that Jesus had a status in his own thought that must be described as that of messiah. If we lift him beyond the prophetic category, strictly speaking, there is no other alternative. That is, there is no other live alternative in his ancient setting. Before we jump to that conclusion, however, we must consider one other fact. That is his humility, especially as it comes to expression in his path to the cross.

In the light of what we have already seen of Jesus' assumption of authority, and related factors, it is not too difficult to understand why he was put to death. He did nothing less than challenge the vested interests of the Jewish leaders at their most sensitive points. That he did so with an emphatic aggressiveness that made it impossible to ignore him made his death a foregone conclusion. The evidence for this exists in many things that have already been set before us, and additional evidence will appear at a later point. We need not review it here. We are more interested in how Jesus himself interpreted this eventuality to himself and in relation to his mission.

The records in this respect have almost certainly been highly interpreted by his disciples. The death of Jesus presented them with a very difficult problem. They were convinced of his innocence and of his vindication by God, but how were they to convince others who viewed the crucifixion as a defeat? The New Testament writers, Paul especially, came forth with theories of an apologetic nature. The Gospel records are part of that apologetic procedure. They are not simply reports of what happened. They are reports of what happened interpreted to the end of justifying Jesus' death. Because of that we cannot always be sure when we are dealing with the mind of Jesus and when we are confronting what his disciples imagined his mind to be. The predictions of the Passion, for example, are too precise to be completely reliable. It is reasonable to think that Jesus anticipated his death. Unless we grant him a foreknowledge greater than a normal human being, however, we cannot accept his reported words as exactly what he said. And there are other indications of legend and of the influence of the tendency to make events coincide with scriptural prediction. Perhaps the most of which we can be certain is that Jesus went to Jerusalem to force a decision regarding himself and his message, as he had previously done in Galilee and its environs. We can believe that he knew how dangerous this was, even that he expected to be repudiated, but it is impossible to ascertain just when this awareness of probable death began to assume serious proportions in his

mind. We can believe that at the Last Supper he said something that
connected his death with God's reign about to be inaugurated, but it
is impossible to know more.

But—what does the record say? What does it suggest that Jesus
was thinking about these events? The record says that, at least in
Jerusalem itself, Jesus anticipated his death. This is the meaning of
the Gethsemane story. At that late hour Jesus was struggling with the
question as to whether or not God really required his death in order
to fulfill his purposes through Jesus. The Passion predictions (Mk.
8:31; 9:31; 10:33 f.) say that before Jesus arrived in Jerusalem he had
premonitions of his fate and that he took it for granted. This is a
reasonable assumption. The fate of John the Baptist, murdered by
Herod Antipas, must have made a profound impression upon Jesus. It
is likely that for one of Jesus' perception the handwriting on the wall
was obvious. If he pursued his goal aggressively, he could not escape
a similar fate. Within that context the struggle in Gethsemane was
the last effort to make certain that such a cruel fate really did serve
the purposes of God. Would it not be wiser to flee and continue his
work beyond the reach of the authorities? Perhaps the cry from the
cross ("My God, my God, why hast thou forsaken me?") is the continuation of the struggle, even though the alternative of escape no
longer exists. It is so easy to think that Jesus must have solved all these
problems easily, when the record says that it was not that way. He
accepted God's will without question, but why should it have been
easier for him than for us to decide exactly what God was asking,
especially in circumstances like that?

What interpretation did Jesus place upon his death? There are
four lines of thought in the Gospels. The first is in line with what has
just been said. He saw it as God's will for him: "The Son of man *must*
suffer." This is probably Christian interpretation, but it is consistent
with Jesus' whole outlook. Everything he taught and did was God's
will as he saw it. His acceptance of the cross could not have been
otherwise. He does not have to have understood fully the reasons for
it in God's mind in order to have accepted it as such.

The second line of thought gives body to the idea that Jesus viewed
his death as God's will for him. "It cannot be that a prophet should
perish away from Jerusalem," Luke reports him as saying. He also had
said something about the killing of the prophets in the past, with the

inference that the Jewish leaders acted in the same way in the present. Apparently he was thinking not only of John the Baptist but also of himself. This indicates an acute sensitivity to the nature of his mission and the strong possibility that what he was trying to do would inevitably lead to a fate like that of his prophetic forebears. The Parable of the Wicked Husbandmen is very pertinent at this point. The absentee landlord sends a series of servants to receive from the tenants the fruits of the vineyard. The tenants abuse some and kill others. Hopefully the landlord sends his own son as his representative. He too is killed. In the light of the treatment of the servants, symbolizing the persecuted prophets, what else was to be expected?

A third line of thought brings out the idea that Jesus viewed his death vicariously as redemptive in its significance. It is remarkable, in the face of later New Testament thought in this direction, that the Gospels have so little to say about it in an explicit way. They record sayings of Jesus in which he asserts that his death is "a ransom for many" and that his blood is "poured out for many." There is also his statement about losing life to save it, and references to service as the supreme mark of greatness. There is, in Luke, Jesus' quotation of Isaiah 61:1–2 in which he equates his ministry with the spirit of the Suffering Servant, but this particular passage does not include the suffering of the Servant. We may take for granted that Jesus viewed his death as a self-giving, as having redemptive significance in his mind. This arises from the whole tenor of his life, however, and not from an abundance of specific sayings of his. The paucity of sayings of a specific nature would suggest that he did not emphasize the idea explicitly.

The fourth line of thought is much more definite in Jesus' words. It is the conviction that God would ultimately vindicate him. He would be crucified, but he would "rise again." That is the form the conviction took in the Passion predictions. It is a fundamental premise of all Jesus' thought that God would ultimately triumph over evil. It was inevitable that he would interpret his repudiation within that context. As God's supreme agent it could not be otherwise. His death was not the end, nor was it a final defeat. The form this vindication would take, as Jesus understood it, is for the moment not relevant. What is important is Jesus' conviction that he was dying in order to live. Out of his dedication to God in the form of the most that a man can give would spring new life for mankind. In that sense vindication was equivalent to vicarious self-giving.

This brings us to the end of the topic. What can we reasonably conclude about the nature of Jesus' authority as he understood it? To look for the answer in the direction of the titles he allegedly employed is futile. We can only guess. Our guess is that he employed several titles, but occasionally and poetically, never as formal or stereotyped designations. He may have used different titles in different circumstances. The term "Son of God" is most consistent with the total impression the records give of his essential attitude and interests. It places the emphasis where he did, that is, on God. His place in God's program had to concern him, but only that he might in thought and action perfectly conform to and represent God's will and purpose. Actually, judging by what we can see, we may question whether Jesus was very much concerned about the question of his designation. He had a task to fulfill, and he assumed an astounding authority in its fulfillment. This came from an intimacy with God beyond our ability to define. That God might be glorified and worshiped through his work was really all that mattered. In life or in death, this was crucial.

The danger of too exclusive a concern with Jesus' status is suggested by a Church historian. He says that the effect of the Christological controversies of the fourth and fifth centuries "was disastrous to church and state." This was not caused by speculation about the person of Jesus. That was inevitable. It was due to the failure of the participants to appreciate the religious and ethical emphases of Jesus as against the finality of any formula of his person. The same warning is implicit in the travesty of much "worship" of Jesus today, perhaps most notably in the so-called Holy Places in his native land. "Not everyone who says to me, 'Lord, Lord,' shall enter the kingdom of heaven, but he who does the will of my Father who is in heaven." That was not only exhortation. It was Jesus' own emphasis with regard to his status and work.

Thus we are directed by him, as well as by logical necessity, to place our emphasis upon the content of his thought. To that task we now turn. It will concern us in the three chapters to follow.

# 3

## GOD THE CREATOR

✜✜✜✜✜✜✜   From the perspective of official Judaism, Jesus was a dangerous radical. He was so menacing to the leaders that they could not feel safe until he had been liquidated. Like most men in their position, they could not foresee the self-defeating results of their actions. They were right at least in their estimate of the implications of Jesus' challenge. From one perspective his work embodied a mighty protest against the institutions of his people. From another perspective, however, it was an attack from within the citadel. It was the revival of the prophetic spirit. It was aimed at calling the People back to its true genius. Innovator though he was, Jesus' message grew out of Hebrew tradition and embodied its best insights. He went beyond anything in his past, but not contrary to it. Thus, as we survey his basic convictions, we become aware of two things at the same time. He takes certain ideas for granted at the same time that he challenges others. The new synthesis he creates is made up of items common to him and his contemporaries. We shall center our attention upon ideas of God. As we do so, this phenomenon will become evident.

God was the sun of Jesus' solar system. Every item of his thought was related to his conception and his experience of God as the planets are related to the sun. Without the sun they would not exist. This is evident in the main theme of Jesus' message, the kingdom (reign) of God. Everything about that reign involved convictions about the existence and the nature of God. This was thoroughly Hebraic. The unique thing about Hebrew and Jewish thought was its conception of God. In analyzing Jesus' thought, it is therefore fitting that we should follow the procedure of concentrating upon this idea and its implications.

The subject will be treated under the three major headings of "God as Creator," "God as Sovereign," and "God as Redeemer." In thought, of course, as in reality, God is all three at the same time. Analysis requires some breakdown, however, and this appears to be the most feasible one. Terms such as "King" or "Father" might be employed, but it seems better to permit them to emerge at relevant places in the discussion than to employ them as chapter headings. The term "Creator" implies Fatherhood, "biologically" considered, as much as the term "Redeemer." Redemptive activity is but one expression of Fatherhood. God as "King" may work for the welfare of his subjects as well as demand obeisance. The terms selected are less ambiguous than "Father" or "King" or some other one.

In developing the theme of each chapter, we shall present a summary picture of relevant background materials, and then proceed to point out ways in which Jesus reacted to his background.

## THE THOUGHT OF JUDAISM

By the time of Jesus the idea of God as Creator was fully taken for granted. It connoted the conviction that the universe in all its forms was completely due to God's creative activity, that it was utterly dependent upon him, and that its future was wholly in his hands. This was a religious rather than a scientific concept. It was a confession of faith, not a speculative deduction from the study of nature and human life. "In the beginning God created the heavens and the earth"—this was Judaism's faith. Typical of the Hebrew manner of reaching conclusions, it had developed out of man's sense of dependence upon God in nature and history. Around the central idea there clustered attitudes of awe and wonder, gratitude, confidence, and complete submission.

Within this context Judaism set its doctrine of man. As created in the image of God, man had dignity. He was superior in value to all other created things:

> Yet thou hast made him little less than God,
> and dost crown him with glory and honor.

Man was the chief object of God's providential care. This explains why Jewish thought gave more attention to human relations in God's sight than to the study of nature. Nature meant little to the Jews as contrasted with the Greeks. One did not look to the hills for help, but beyond them: "My help comes from the Lord who made heaven and earth." God's power was available to man, man who was God's main concern.

To be sure, Adam's error in the Fall had caused God to alter his original scheme. Death and sin had been introduced to mar the original splendor of the Creation. Yet not until after Jesus' time did a doctrine of original sin develop in certain circles. It was not part of his heritage of thought. Man's nature was limited by death and the capacity for sin, but this was not the same thing as congenital corruption. Created in God's image, man had potentialities for goodness as well as for evil; he had a good as well as an evil nature. If man chose to be disobedient to God, God would not stop him or alter the retribution to follow. Retribution was thus the effect of a misuse of freedom, the judgment of God, not caused by incapacity for goodness. Hebrew thought was not speculative in this as in other respects. It simply observed man's mistakes and their consequences, and attributed them to his wrong choices with reference to God's will. The assumptions of modern psychotherapy about human nature, some of them at least, would have had hard sledding in that setting.

With these basic ideas in mind let us consider two major facets of the conception of God as Creator. The first is monotheism, the belief in one God. This distinguished Jewish thought from that of all surrounding nations. It is the glory of Israel, its unique contribution to human thought. Long before Jesus' time it had become the first article of the Confession of Faith: "Hear, O Israel: The Lord our

God, the Lord is one." In the synagogue liturgy it is further elaborated:

> Blessed art thou, O Lord,
> The Most High God, Maker of heaven and earth,
> Our Shield and the Shield of our fathers!
>
> .   .   .   .   .   .   .   .   .   .   .   .
>
> Holy art thou and terrible is thy Name,
> And there is no God beside thee.

This point need not be labored. We should, however, note two things that monotheism meant to Judaism with reference to ideas current in the world at that time.

It was a complete repudiation of polytheism, the belief in several gods. For the Jew there were no other gods; there was only God. Since idols stood for what did not exist, they were anathema. Idolatry became the greatest crime, representing the worship as God of that which was less than God. There might be other beings, messengers and servants of God, but they were always less than and subordinate to God. He had no rivals.

The second distinctive meaning monotheism had is related to this idea. If there was but one God, an unmodified dualism could not be assumed as an explanation of the existence of evil in the world. Some thinkers, especially in Persia, contended that evil existed apart from God and was caused by a Competitor of equal status. Jewish thought was influenced to some extent by this type of explanation, but it always insisted that such dualism conform to a monotheistic premise. Only a modified dualism could exist on that basis. If evil was in any sense due to an agent other than God, he existed only because God permitted it, and he would ultimately be eliminated by God. He was at best a temporary instrument in God's hands to serve his mysterious ends.

The other facet of God as Creator that should be elaborated with reference to Jesus' day was the doctrine of transcendence, or the "otherness" of God. In the speculation of the schoolmen this idea was receiving great emphasis. The doctrine asserted that God was invisible and completely out of man's reach or control, transcending the world and the universe. He could not be comprehended ration-

ally as in Greek thought. He was unapproachably holy. The idea of the
Holy had strong ethical connotations, as in Isaiah's vision when his
sight of the King, high and lifted up, drove him to his knees. It also
contained more primitive elements of taboo, as illustrated by the
stories of the giving of the Covenant at Sinai. The people avoided
too close contact with the holy mountain lest they violate the taboo.
However one might interpret the nature of God's holiness, it did not
mean that he was completely inaccessible. It did mean that he was
supremely majestic and unique in character. Because of this there
was a tendency to avoid the use of the divine Name. Circumlocutions
were used instead: "The Blessed," "The Name," "The Word," and
so forth. This led also to great care in following scrupulously the
divinely dictated regulations for temple worship. The high ritualist
usually emerges out of such an atmosphere.

There had been a day when God in the form of a man came into
Eden to communicate with his creatures, but those days were long
gone. Skeptics were reminded that even Moses had not been permitted to see God's face.

Two aspects of this situation call for special attention. One concerns the Jewish doctrine of revelation. God's revelation of his will
was assumed to have been an act of grace on his part. He desired to
provide man with guidance in the midst of a perplexing existence.
Potentially this revelation was designed for all men, but Israel alone
had been truly receptive to it. This broader conception is implied in
the existence of pre-Mosaic commandments allegedly communicated
to Noah. Paul knows of their existence and appears to have them in
mind in Romans. The narrower view prevailed in Jesus' time, however, constituting the theory of a "special revelation" to God's people.
This consisted of the Torah (Law) and its Oral Tradition ("a fence
around the Law"), along with the recorded words of prophets and
teachers.

This doctrine was consistent with, as it implied, the idea of God's
transcendence. The basic conviction was that God had in the past
revealed himself in a Book, the scriptures, and that the period of
revelation was past. God was present, in an external and impersonal
way, in his past revelation—a sort of absentee landlord. The prophetic
voice, directly stimulated by God's Word within his heart, was no
longer heard in the land. The revelation given in the Book was final

and complete, except for the interpretations of its meaning by the scribes. This interpretation, the Oral Tradition, was itself considered to have been revealed implicitly to Moses along with the written Torah. In this way a Book of History was transformed into a Book of Law.

Related to this and implying the same thing in a different way was the dualism of what is called apocalyptic thought. This was a type of thought that asserted that the world was so evil and men so disobedient that God would soon destroy it. More precisely, it was a way in which some Jewish thinkers strove to solve the problem of evil created by the contrast between the high hopes of the Jews and their actual circumstances. We shall deal more fully with this subject later. For the moment we simply observe the way in which it both implied and embodied the premises of the doctrine of transcendence. Essentially it said that God had acted in the past and that he would assert himself in the future but that he had for all practical purposes suspended his activity in the present.

Attempts speculatively to bridge the gulf between the transcendent God and lowly man led to the supposition that God employed subordinate beings as his messengers. One form of this was the doctrine of angels, especially apparent in apocalyptic thought (for a Christian example consider The Revelation to John). In Jesus' day angelology became greatly elaborated. Names familiar to us, such as Gabriel and Michael, were assigned to certain leading angels at this time, and they were grouped in a hierarchy. One of the sources of this doctrine is related to the prevailing monotheism. Foreign gods were not eliminated, but demoted to the status of angels or messengers of the one God. Another speculative turn fastened upon abstract ideas such as Spirit, Word of God, and Wisdom. They were made more concrete in the form of personifications of divine activities and powers. A parallel process took place in Greece when the ancient gods were transformed into personifications of divine attributes. With direct reference to the doctrine of creation, Wisdom received more attention than Spirit and Word. It had an international flavor in its earlier history, but in Jesus' day it was made to conform to the narrower view that prevailed. It became more Jewish, and was even identified with the Torah.

This type of thought did not permeate all areas of Judaism. It was

largely confined to the schools. The basic premises with regard to
God's revelation of his will in the Torah, however, were widely held
and respected. Judaism at that time was the People of the Book. And
this rested upon, as it supported, the idea of God's majesty and
uniqueness embodied in the thought of his transcendent holiness.

Allegiance to the doctrine might, however, be more formal than
vital for some. There was a much warmer and more vital religious life
in Judaism than this might suggest. Nor was it confined to those outside the circles of the schools. Among the scribes themselves it existed. This may appear to be a contradiction, but we may recall that
one outstanding characteristic of Hebrew thought was its lack of
complete logical consistency. There were experiences of the Shekina,
that is, of direct communications from God, even though they were
spasmodic. God's Word was not confined to the Book despite the
theory of revelation. There was a vitality of religious life that the
Psalms exemplify and that was also operative in synagogue worship
in some respects. There was the memory of the prophets as well as
of the Law, and the sensitive heart would respond to it. Private prayer
and synagogue prayer assumed that God not only knew and cared
but that he was near and approachable. Transcendent he might be,
but he was also near. If that was not possible on the basis of strict
logic, so much the worse for logic! The Jew would not even have
understood the objection.

What his heart did understand, as his experience taught him, were
sentiments such as:

> Whither shall I go from thy Spirit?
> Or whither shall I flee from thy presence?
> If I ascend to heaven, thou art there!
> If I make my bed in Sheol, thou art there!

or,

> Even though I walk through the valley of the shadow of death,
> I fear no evil;
> for thou art with me;

or,

God is our refuge and strength,
a very present help in trouble.
Therefore we will not fear though the earth should change,
though the mountains shake in the heart of the sea.

God was the Creator, and he might well be as far away as some of
the schoolmen said. Surely he was mighty and majestic, omnipo-
tent, omniscient, perfectly holy. But—he had not forgotten the purpose of his creation of man in his image. One might have to wait
to see this purpose fulfilled, perhaps until God intervened to end
history, but in the meantime he was at work. He was immanent as
well as transcendent. So some at least thought. If some tended to
believe that God's will was set forth only, or primarily, in his Word
from the past, there were others who knew in their hearts that he
still spoke.

## THE REACTIONS OF JESUS

In its essential features the picture of Jewish thought that has
been portrayed is that of Jesus. This applies particularly to the general conception of creation, including the doctrine of man, and to
monotheism. Jesus took these ideas for granted. It applies also to the
thought of God's transcendence, although Jesus modified this idea
in significant ways. We shall survey Jesus' thought briefly in areas of
agreement, with some attention to his emphases, and elaborate more
fully the way in which he reacted to the idea of God's transcendence.

What one takes for granted he does not emphasize. It exists as
a presupposition of thought that manifests itself by implication. This
is the case with Jesus' ideas about the creation. On one occasion he
uses the expression "from the beginning of creation," but even if he
hadn't we would know that he accepted fully orthodox Jewish doctrine in its general features. It was for him, as for others, a confession
of faith, a predominantly religious conception. To the extent that
he gave any attention to nature, as against human relations, a sensitivity to small and minute things is revealed. God operated in the
growing seed. His beauty could be observed in the wild flowers. He
knew when a sparrow fell. This was a microscopic vision as against a
telescopic vision. In the Old Testament, generally speaking, God's

activity in the field of nature was seen in large and dramatic events: thunder and lightning at Sinai, plagues and a path through the sea, storms delivering the Israelites at Megiddo or saving Elijah's face in the presence of the priests of Baal. For Jesus the stress fell upon a mustard seed and birds lodging in the limbs of the full-grown bush. There is more to this than appears on the surface. It bears directly upon the idea of God's transcendence, as we shall see, and upon much else besides. It implies that in Jesus' thought nothing was too small to escape God's attention. There is the implication of a direct dealing with everything rather than the distant touch of an absentee landlord. The God who had created the heavens and the earth, in whose hands was the destiny of his universe, took note of the hairs of our heads.

Judaism's doctrine of man was taken over by Jesus with little change. Man had a unique dignity in God's sight. He had tremendous potentialities as made in God's image. He could have fellowship with God. Jesus was realistic about man's capacity for sin. Man could bring himself by persistent disobedience into a state that could only be described as unforgivable. Yet, the door of repentance and of forgiveness remained open, if he wished to rise to his true condition as man made in God's image. Jesus did not hold a doctrine of original sin. The only indication of such a view is a chance phrase ("you who are evil"), upon the basis of which a doctrine can hardly be constructed. Jesus' outlook was an optimistic one regarding the potentialities of human nature. He would hardly have emphasized repentance as he did, if he thought man could not do anything about it. Nor would he have taken his own vocation so seriously, and sought others to join him, if he thought that human efforts were of no avail.

The emphasis of Jesus in this area falls upon the supreme value of man over against qualifying conditions set up in the practice of legalism. It is summed up in his statement, "The sabbath is made for man, not man for the sabbath." Regulations for the Sabbath must be designed to elevate man's essential dignity, not subordinate it to institutionalism or any other instrumental value. His constant association with "publicans and sinners," despised by the respectable of his society, brings this out. There are standards for judging the worth of men other than those of legalism.

Jesus also gave an exaggerated turn to the thought of God's providence, to the idea of his constant and beneficent care for his creation. His rain falls upon just and unjust alike. Anxiety has no place in a situation in which the flowers of the field and the birds of the air bespeak their creator's beneficence. If a father, asked by his son for bread, will not give him a stone, how much more reliable is God? Daily bread is a fit subject for prayer. Knowing our needs before we ask, God constantly seeks to make power available. Like leaven, he is at work in his creation to bring his Spirit to man and to sustain him in life. There is warmth in this view of the Creator, even extravagance in picturing his providential care.

Monotheism was obviously the assumption of Jesus. His theme was the reign of God, one and not several. When he quoted the Shema—"Hear, O Israel: The Lord our God, the Lord is one"—he was as orthodox as the Christian who recites the first article of the Apostles' Creed: "I believe in God the Father Almighty, Maker of heaven and earth." He was as much a monotheist as the Muslim extolling Allah. The Muslim in fact got his monotheism from the Hebrews. In assuming this conception of God, Jesus too repudiated polytheism and an unmodified dualism in the Godhead. What distinguished Jesus' grasp of this conception was the intensity and the seriousness with which he took its moral implications. This distinguishes his thought as a whole, and in dealing with its various facets we shall by implication be elaborating his monotheistic view of God. Among other things, we shall observe the universalistic aspects of his outlook. Who were his mother and his brothers? Who were God's People? The answer is the same in each case: "Whoever does the will of God." Whoever does the will of God, that is, as Jesus understood that will. What he thought about that will eventually appear in the course of our treatment, and the question need not be discussed further here.

It is with regard to the doctrine of God's transcendence that Jesus' variations from Jewish views are best observed. That is, variations from the views of some. Generally speaking, he stood with those for whom the religion of the heart was the vital thing. As such he remained within Judaism even as he qualified certain of its views. Let us be more precise.

He took for granted the thought that God was transcendent. This was implicit in his acceptance of the doctrine of creation. This appears incidentally rather than explicitly in his sayings. God is "Lord of heaven and earth." Heaven is his throne and earth his footstool. All things are possible to him. Above all, he is absolutely and perfectly holy. He alone is good, being perfect. As compared with the best parent in his care for his child, God is superior. Before his face every man is an unworthy servant, his most superb achievement of character or piety being but a pale shadow of the glory that is God. Thus men are not even to swear by facets of his creation. Every approach to him must be in the spirit of "Hallowed be thy name."

With all that, Jesus did not carry the idea to unreasonable extremes. He believed in the "otherness" of God, but that was only part of the story. It was not even the most important part. Jesus avoided the peril of considering God so transcendent as to be abstract, with no value for living. He existed above his universe in primary respects, yet he was not an absentee landlord. Nor did Jesus go to the other extreme. He did not consider God sentimentally or with disrespect. He never sacrificed his absolute character as Lord of heaven and earth and as absolute Holiness. What Jesus did was to emphasize the paradoxical idea that the absolutely transcendent and holy Creator also draws near to man, without sacrificing any of his glory. This is the significance of the term "Father" as applied to God. It was as Father that he created man, with loving concern and care, and with every intention of accepting full responsibility for this act. Thus he could not leave man entirely to himself.

The immanence, or nearness, of God, as Jesus viewed it, comes out in several ways with great emphasis in his sayings. It is in fact the presupposition of practically everything he teaches. It is suggested in a negative way by the fact that Jesus does not speculate, as the schoolmen did, about the nature of creation. He takes for granted the doctrine of angels, but beyond that he does not concern himself with speculation about hypostases or personifications of divine attributes. His spirit is foreign to such theological reasoning. He was not of the schools, but of the people. It is the premise of his authority, as that subject has been treated in the preceding chapter. It is fundamental to his idea of the reign of God, which will be discussed in the next chapter. We shall not elaborate this idea here, thus avoiding needless repetition. We shall simply point out a few illustrations of the fact that will appear in other forms later.

Four specific aspects of Jesus' thought are sufficient to clarify the matter and to show what he emphasized. He was not reluctant to pronounce the divine Name, but the term he chose was that of "Father" (Aramaic: "Abba"). With this title he addressed God and told his disciples to do likewise. The term stood for God in his capacity as Creator as well as Redeemer, but Jesus gave it the warmth it had in the circles of Judaism from which came such an expression as, "Like as a Father pitieth his children, so the Lord pitieth them that fear him." He stressed its family connotations. As Father, God loved his children. God's forgiving love will be dealt with at a later point. The general conception is all that we need to consider at the moment. The conception implies more than warmth in God's attitude toward men. It implies his presence and his activity to the ends of man's welfare in the present.

The distribution of the term "Father" among the sources of Jesus' sayings raises a question that should be considered. It appears seldom in Mark and Q (material common to Matthew and Luke) and L (material peculiar to Luke). It is abundant in M (material peculiar to Matthew). Its most frequent use is in John, going far beyond the total usage in the first three Gospels. The implication of this is that Jesus used the title much less frequently than John's Gospel suggests. If so, the explanation may serve our purpose. One interpretation is that the idea of God as Father was as much a presupposition of Jesus' thought as was his monotheism. He did not need to emphasize the one more than the other. He simply took it for granted. If so, this indicates how profoundly he assumed God's care and his nearness. At least God was such a reality as Father that he could not be conceived as an absentee landlord who had to delegate to intermediate beings his responsibility to his creatures. He could thus be addressed directly, provided the title was one of respect and appreciation.

A second mark of Jesus' emphasis upon the immanence of God was the simplicity of his praying. Nothing could be more direct or more simple than the Lord's Prayer. This is typical of Jesus' whole manner in approaching God and of his teaching about prayer. He is most explicit on this subject when he criticizes those who pray in public to get attention, practicing their piety before men, and who think that elaborate formulas are required in order to secure God's favorable response. The latter implies the thought that God is remote and also fussy about correct procedures of a liturgical nature in the approach to him. Although on a very high religious and ethical level, "The Eighteen Benedictions," typical of prayer in the synagogues, shares something of this elaboration as compared with the Lord's Prayer. All that was required, said Jesus, was sincerity and realism. Prayer was sincere if it was addressed to God, without thought for observers. To enter into one's closet for prayer was not a stage direction. It was a way of saying that man must shut out all distractions and concentrate upon God. Realism dictated the thought that God was immediately available, requiring no elaborate ritual. This applied in the direction of temple sacrifice as well. Apparently Jesus did not frown upon worship in the temple. In cleansing the temple he simply demanded that worship be genuine, without commercialism and without exclusiveness: "My house shall be called a house of *prayer* for *all* nations." He was not carrying on a campaign against liturgy and ritualism as such. He asked only that it be sincere and genuine in its practice and effects. At the same time he had no sympathy with the trend that emphasized scrupulous and meticulous concern for ritualistic details of sacrifice and worship, such as was the result of carrying to extremes the idea of God's transcendence. In this way he qualified that conception too.

But, in the third place, he went much further. He was not content simply to assert that God was approachable and available in sincere and realistic prayer and worship. He said that God took the initiative in seeking men. Like the shepherd whose lamb had gone astray, God sought men until he found them. He was "The Hound of Heaven," never content to let men be at peace in their service of values less than absolute values, that is, of God himself. Thus Jesus associated himself with the sinners, whether they were morally sinful or careless of ritualistic niceties. Thus he went to the hated tax collectors, even making one of them an intimate disciple. God was like that, he implied. His view of God's judgment has a finality about it that leaves no room for repentance after it is passed, but, viewed in conjunction with God's love, it too served the ends of God's love. God would not let man rest, in heart or in social relationships, unless he was at peace with God. In holding to this view of the divine initiative, Jesus stood at the opposite extreme from those who exaggerated the idea of God's transcendence or who failed to balance it by means of qualifying considerations.

Finally, we can almost anticipate the way in which Jesus qualified the doctrine of revelation that was current in Judaism. This has already been set before us in the previous chapter. Theoretically Jesus held the doctrine of the origin and the significance of the Torah that was orthodox Judaism in his time. By implication, however, he denied it. He did find God speaking to him in scripture, to be sure, but in a much more creative manner than the legalist, on the basis of his premises, could even imagine. The only "special revelation" Jesus knew anything about was one with revelation in general. In the prophetic mold Jesus believed that God spoke directly to the conscience and the heart of man. If man was to discover his Word in scripture, he must come with a mind prepared to understand and perceive it. In that process he would not find God equally revealed in every part of scripture, but only on its highest levels. On the basis of this presupposition, Jesus was convinced that God was revealing himself in his mind with a new and dynamic significance for his contemporaries. This point need not be elaborated beyond what has already been said. This was Jesus' final and conclusive way of qualifying the doctrine of God's transcendence in its extreme form. It is this that leads one scholar to write, "The revelation of God in Christ is not the imparting of a new idea of God; it is a fresh unveiling of the Reality to which ideas, new and old, with greater or less accuracy apply." Because Jesus listened to God's voice within, he discriminated between ideas and values set forth in the Book and in contemporary thought, and thus he was able to embody them in a life that in and of itself is God's revelation in its ultimate dimensions.

The way in which Jesus, while standing upon the shoulders of his Hebrew past, transcended that heritage without departing from its boundaries has been depicted in this chapter in one of its facets. There are others as well. The next two chapters will describe them.

# 4

## GOD THE SOVEREIGN

❖❖❖❖❖❖❖ It has been implied that as Creator God was in control of his universe. How this idea worked itself out with reference to the people he had brought into being concerns us in this chapter. The subject breaks down into three topics: its political meaning, the problem of evil, and the nature of God's demands. Jewish legalism in Jesus' time is a prominent feature of the third topic.

### THE THOUGHT OF JUDAISM

The thought of Judaism regarding God's sovereignty is defined by the term "theocracy." This means direct rule by God in contrast to government by an earthly king (autocracy), a wealthy class (plutocracy), the people (democracy), or other alternatives. It is a religious conception with political connotations. It means that a holy People, a Church-State, which acknowledges God alone as King, accepts his reign on earth through the agency of divinely chosen priests who administer his affairs. The priests come to their places of leadership by heredity. The prophet has his place in this regime. He is one selected by God to bring a specific message to the People in extraordinary circumstances. In the past the prophets had served to restrain tendencies toward tyranny and worship of foreign gods when the form of government moved toward autocracy under David, Solomon, and their successors. Israel had never really been happy with her kings. This view explains the resentment on the part of the Jews toward the Roman overlord in the time of Jesus, and especially toward Herod the Great and his sons. Because they treated the office of high priest as a political football, they were viewed as usurpers of prerogatives that belonged alone to God.

The idea of the Kingship of God is as old as the nation itself. The emphasis falls upon the absoluteness of his sovereignty. He is the sole ruler of the universe and everyone in it. The term "kingdom of God" is not a prominent one in the Old Testament and Jewish literature, but the idea is basic to their thought. "Kingdom" in this connection should be translated "reign" or "rulership." It is one of the accidents of history that a particular form of government provided the specific term by means of which to designate God's sovereignty. After the Babylonian Exile it was the priests who were considered to be the rulers of the People, acting for God. Even the expected messiah was but an agent of God, a figurehead, to do his bidding. Much thought of God's future triumph did not include a messianic figure at all. It was believed that God would act directly and alone, accompanied by a multitude of subordinate beings.

The idea of theocracy rested upon two fundamental pillars, the Election and the Covenant. It was believed that God had chosen Israel to be his People and to fulfill his purposes in history in a special way. He had done this by a historical act, selecting Moses as his agent. This Election in the past had been a sheer act of grace. It was not dictated by any unusual merit upon the part of the forefathers or of those who were the subjects of election. God had simply chosen Israel rather than any other nation as the instrument of his will. The story of Moses and the Exodus in the scriptures made this clear, and it was supported by many other indications in the sacred writings.

The Election was cemented by the Covenant. It stated the conditions upon the basis of which the relationship was to exist. The demands upon the People were few and simple, but of crucial importance. God's favor depended upon loyalty to them. He was capable of inflicting severe penalties if they were violated. At first the Covenant was narrow in scope. It was restricted to the nation as such. The People of God were the people of Israel. In the course of time profounder moral insights broadened its scope. This was primarily the contribution of the classical Hebrew prophets of the eighth and seventh centuries B.C. They introduced the shocking thought that God could reject his People for unfaithfulness to his moral requirements. This broadened the scope of God's sovereignty. It also brought into being the idea that a faithful Remnant was in essence God's People, not the political unit as such.

In Jesus' time the most burning issue was that of the meaning of the Covenant in this connection. The older, more exclusive conception had never been completely eliminated. In the Judaism of the first century the idea of the Remnant was even interpreted along this line. Israel was the "Saved Remnant," both ritualistically and morally defined, in an exclusive sense. Others followed to its logical conclusion the implications of prophetic thought. To them Israel was the "Saving Remnant," the emphasis falling upon her responsibility to bring God's light to the nations. This conflict in view was that of nationalist and internationalist. In either case the idea of divine Election combined with that of the Covenant relationship to define the conception of theocracy which dominated Jewish thinking.

Prophetic ideas caused another problem to arise, the problem of evil. It became acute in the period following the Babylonian Exile. Inspired by Ezekial and Isaiah of the Exile (Is. 40 ff.), some of the Hebrew aliens in Babylon returned to Jerusalem. They set up a theocratic form of government and life. They attempted to meet the conditions of the Covenant faithfully. They could no longer believe that God's sovereignty was confined to them, but they knew themselves to be his special charges. Furthermore, the idea of his justice was emphatic in their thought. On that basis they tended to conclude that God should give them preferential treatment. This was, however, contradicted by the facts of experience. Israel did not become dominant over other nations. She was not even permitted to exist unmolested and to work out her theocracy. Instead she suffered the outrages of foreign conquest and persecution. The problem was also acute on the personal level. It was assumed that God rewarded goodness and punished evil in this life. This was the doctrine of retribution in a period when no idea of a future life existed. But, as Job indicates, things did not seem to work out that way.

With reference to the fate of the People as a whole, less than two hundred years before the birth of Jesus the nation had been shaken to its foundations by the Syrian ruler Antiochus IV Epiphanes (deity manifested). His intention was to destroy Judaism by introducing Hellenistic customs and ways of life, although his basic interest was probably to unite the Hellenistic states. The penalty for violating his demands was death. The Maccabees successfully resisted this threat. They succeeded in restoring both religious and political autonomy, but this was short-lived. Herod the Great and the Romans soon destroyed what the Maccabees had built up. The religious autonomy of the Jews was left intact, but politically they became subservient to the foreigner. The high priests were appointed and removed at will. To the Jews this appeared to be a very unjust way for God to treat them. It became necessary to think through the meaning of God's justice in such circumstances.

A minority view was that God was through this suffering disciplining the People to its primary task of converting mankind. It is the view of many Jews today who oppose political Zionism. The more popular means of overcoming the dilemma was that of apocalypticism. This transferred to the future judgment the balancing of the scales of justice. Along with it came the idea of resurrection in Pharisaic thought, and also an emphasis upon individual rewards and punishments. The basic thought was that, whatever the signs to the contrary, God had not deserted his People or any given individual. In his own good time, sooner rather than later, he would end human history and reward those who had in this life suffered unjustly. Thus the ways of God with man were justified.

This type of thought will be elaborated more fully later. For the moment the point is that the sovereignty of God, ethically interpreted, was maintained by an emphasis upon a future judgment. Although this was a development beyond previous thought in several ways, it was consistent with the fundamental Hebrew view of history. This view believed that history was moving toward a goal, like an arrow shot at a target. God had created the world with a purpose that he intended to fulfill in history. This differed from the idea of history as a series of cycles, as in Greek thought with its symbol of the hoop snake. Apocalypticism held to this basic idea, but it changed the terminal point from a victory within history to the end of history. The Lord of history became One who brought history to a cataclysmic conclusion. This did not alter the fundamental premise of the Hebrew philosophy of history. Only its form was changed.

There were other solutions of the problem of evil, usually more with reference to the fate of individuals than of the nation. There was the solution of Job and Psalm 73. Peace was found in the consciousness of being "near God" without a specific explanation of misfortune. A more sophisticated answer was that of Ecclesiastes. In an agnostic and pessimistic spirit it simply sought to make the best of a bad mess, affirming no more than that "all is vanity," "the clouds return after the rain." This was not unlike Stoic ideas. As has been said, there was the answer of Isaiah of the Exile. Those who followed this line of thought would have led the nation toward a conception of redemptive suffering as a means of bringing "light to the Gentiles." The synagogue ritual in certain respects reflected this spirit. However, these were minority voices in the face of apocalypticism. We cannot be certain as to the exact extent or influence of this latter outlook, but we can confidently believe that it was the solution most easily accepted by a great many.

Underlying all these variations of thought there persisted the fundamental conviction that God was the absolute ruler of the universe and that he would ultimately bring his purposes to fulfillment. The arrow would reach its target—without any doubt, because God was Creator and King. This sovereignty was basically a religious concept taking politically the form of theocracy in Judaism. It was this-worldly in perspective. It was defined by the Covenant and the Law as a way of life in which, both ritualistically and ethically, the People served God and dealt with outsiders. At the same time, owing to the problem of evil, it became increasingly evident that the ideal was unrealizable in this life. Thus the thought of a future judgment arose in suprahistorical terms. The Jews might disagree upon the form which God's triumph would take, but on the fact itself there was no disagreement or doubt.

We may now turn to the question of just what it was that God demanded of his People. How were good and evil defined? God demanded absolute obedience. This was to take the form of a righteous life. Loyalty in this respect was to be as complete as the sacrificial victim on the temple altars, entire and without blemish. "Righteousness," however, was an inclusive term for conduct pleasing to God. It meant faithfulness to his commandments. It was as general and as much an omnibus term as its opposite, "unrighteousness" or "evil." It served a purpose in this foundational respect. It defined sin as at root disobedience to God. It thus had a reference to idolatry, the worship of something relative as though it were an absolute. As Paul wrote about the Gentiles, "they did not honor him as God, . . . they served the creature rather than the Creator." Self-worship was its worst form. With all that, the content of "righteousness" still needed explication and elaboration.

For Judaism this was provided by the Torah (law, precept, revelation, divine instruction). The theory assumed was that God was the perfect Lawgiver. He had given the Torah for Israel's guidance as an act of grace. Obedience to it was the main evidence of gratitude and the mark of loyalty to God. The Torah was for Judaism not just law in general, even though it was all-inclusive. It contained rules for "secular" living as well as a Rule of Faith. It combined religious and ethical precepts with rules of public health and even of manners. It was considered to be revelation, divine instruction, communicated to Moses and specially selected servants. Thus it was not subject to ratification like a constitutional amendment. It was to be accepted, not debated and voted upon. It was of course irrevocable on that premise. Its precepts could not be altered, and no substitution could be made for any one. They might be interpreted with reference to specific conditions, even added to in line with their basic intent, but that was all.

As one would expect, everything in the Torah had a religious orientation. Judaism knew nothing of the type of thought today that rears an ethical system on the basis of standards and values arising out of society without reference to an objective external order. In that sense a Jew in Jesus' day could not have been a Communist or an atheistic humanist in any form. Righteousness was defined by God in his revealed Torah. It was a social righteousness to be realized in a social order. In that respect it was like some Greek thought. For the latter the social ideal was the city-state, while for Judaism it was the People of God. The difference was that Judaism emphasized the divine origin of the definition of the rules by which the people were to live.

Becoming more specific, Judaism was taught that God required the observance of the *whole* Torah, including its interpretation by the scribes called the Oral Tradition (or Tradition of the Elders). This meant to make no distinction between positive and negative, moral and ceremonial, precepts, nor to arrange the precepts in order of importance. It was to be respected and obeyed in all its parts. Ever since the time of Ezra following the Babylonian Exile, this had been the distinguishing mark of Judaism. They were the People of the Book. In Jesus' day this was the prevailing view of leadership in both temple and synagogue. The priests were the chief instruments of enforcing the Law. The scribes served as lawyers and interpreters. Temple worship was regulated by the Torah. Synagogue worship, nonsacrificial in nature and less strictly legalistic, was also devoted to it. As compared with the pagan neighbors of the Jews, the unique aspect of all this was the attempt to regulate life in the present by a record of past events recorded in a Book.

This created difficulties the scribes sought to overcome by their interpretations. It was not always easy to see the relevance to present conditions of a precept that had arisen in quite different social and cultural circumstances. Laws for an agricultural community did not without some ingenuity in interpretation suit urban conditions. Furthermore, although past events were considered to be important, viewing a Book of History as primarily a Book of Law tended to qualify a realistic view of history. This is what happened in another direction, as we have seen. Apocalypticism tended to change God from Lord of history to One who would end history.

The whole Torah was to be observed. That was the theory. However, even the most severe literalists choose within the Bible that which they wish to emphasize. So it was in Judaism. Certain precepts were given more prominence than others. Among these were those relative to the annual festivals centering in temple worship, with great care being given to proper forms of sacrifice and offerings. Male Jews were expected to attend at least one such festival each year. Earlier, three visits had been required. These festivals arose originally in connection with agricultural interests, but over the years their character had changed. In Jesus' time they had come to have patriotic significance, religiously oriented, like Memorial Day or the Fourth of July in the United States. The Passover commemorated the Exodus when the nation had been formed under Moses. The Feast of Weeks commemorated the giving of the Torah at Mount Sinai. The Feast of Tabernacles (Tents) looked back to the time when Israel had dwelt in tents in the wilderness preparatory to making the conquest of the Promised Land. And there were others. These feasts were very different from those of pagan religions in one fundamental respect. The latter celebrated the doings of gods in an imaginary mythology. The feasts of Judaism rested upon a historical memory. The Passover reminded the people of something that had actually happened, just as the Fourth of July does in America. To that extent, despite the qualifications previously cited, God was the Lord of history for Judaism.

Certain ritual matters were also emphasized. Among many others, three stood out: Circumcision, the Sabbath, and Tithes. Each in its own way was a badge or symbol of the Jew's dedication to God. Circumcision marked him indelibly as a member of the Elect People. Sabbath observance symbolized the total consecration of his work and effort to God. The regular giving of tithes ("a fence around riches") symbolized a comparable consecration of his possessions and earnings. Much more can be said about what was required by the Torah in ritual terms, but this is sufficient to clarify the basic nature of the requirements.

With particular reference to Jesus' reactions, it is necessary to elaborate somewhat the description of the legalistic way in which this "system" operated. Any religious discipline based on law becomes legalistic. By its nature it is legalistic. It differs considerably from the approach of the prophet to religious and ethical questions. Prophetic religion is more concerned with right motivation out of which right living emerges as fruit from a tree. It views the soul as a seed to be cultivated. The legalist thinks of the soul as a cistern to be filled. Moral precepts are more significant to the prophet than ritual precepts. First century Judaism theoretically stressed the importance of right motive and it was concerned with morality. What mattered, however, was conduct in conformity with the Torah, and ritual prescriptions were as important as moral ones. It was a system of military discipline, conformity enforced by external pressure. The good man was one who conformed, even though it might be assumed that his heart should go along with the external compulsion. Legalism sought to cover every possible contingency of conduct with a specific rule. All that one had to do was to look up the rule in the Book and observe it. The Oral Tradition served this purpose. It developed a maze of regulations in interpreting the meaning of the basic written Torah. Six hundred and thirteen basic biblical laws were listed, covering the most trivial as well as the most important matters. The scribe was required by the ordinary layman for guidance through this wilderness. By contrast the prophet dispensed with all this. When a man's heart was right, he said, when it was informed with sentiments of justice and love, his intelligence would guide him to right conclusions in specific circumstances. This approach was creative, not static. It assumed a dignity in man that the legalistic system did not. Two different ideas of God were presupposed. For the prophet, God spoke directly to the heart and the conscience. For the legalist, an Absentee Landlord had handed down his dictates in a Book. The legalist might well be better than his system, as many were, but the differences between his conceptions and those of the prophet still stand.

The jungle of tangled regulations in the Oral Tradition may be illustrated by those relative to Sabbath observance. The Torah commanded that the Sabbath be kept holy, and work was prohibited. But—what was work? Thirty-nine classes of work were declared to be illegal, each with many subdivisions. Among others were the following: sowing, plowing, reaping, tying a knot, loosening a knot, sewing two stitches, tearing in order to sew two stitches, writing two letters, erasing in order to write two letters, lighting a fire, building. Things got really complex when questions arose about details. For example, what was plowing? Was it confined to making a furrow in the usual way, or did it include an inadvertent scraping of the earth with a stick? The Oral Tradition tried to answer all such questions, at infinitely monotonous length. This was its nature with regard to every minute facet of conduct, both ritual and ethical, religious and secular.

There are built-in liabilities in any legalistic structure, and Judaism illustrates them all. Correct procedure in ritual matters being as important as moral living, a sense of proportion is lost. The multiplication of minute regulations leads to an overscrupulous splitting of hairs. One forgets the wood for the trees. Formal obedience replaces creative or radical obedience. The voice of God in heart and conscience is smothered. The dynamic nature of true faith and repentance tends to be lost. They become meritorious works rather than expressions of God's forgiving grace. Self-righteousness results as one judges his strictness in observing the rules as superior to that of another, especially if he does more than the law explicitly exacts. He may do all this and still be cold of heart in the face of human need. This system offers no power by which to achieve what it requires. It makes room for forgiveness, but its ultimate means of salvation is an impossible perfect performance. Thus it condemns rather than inspires. It offers a social gospel, an ordering of society by legislation, but it does not give enough attention to motivation or the problem of individual salvation. It clutters up the social scene with dead wood when circumstances require revision of the laws, since nothing may be discarded.

This in theory was the prevailing situation in Judaism. However, few adhere with complete strictness to such a rigid pattern. Legalism was qualified in any number of ways in Jesus' day. It was actually only the crust, the outer surface of a vital religious life on the part of many. Some apparently demonstrated almost all the defects of legalism, but there were many who did not. The fence the leaders tried to erect around Judaism, in order to protect the basic commandments, sagged in many places and was completely broken down at others. Even the most ardent defenders of the system qualified their theory in practice.

The principle of *Erub* is a good illustration of the way in which strict legalism was qualified within the legal structure itself. What this principle permitted was legal, but it was a sort of mental gymnastics that in reality denied the fundamental presupposition of the Law. It encouraged a legal fiction in order to preserve a presupposition that could not be fulfilled. The *Erub* was a symbolical act by means of which the spirit rather than the letter of the Law might be observed. For example, the Oral Tradition set up definite restrictions upon movements upon the Sabbath. One was permitted to go only a certain distance from his home or from wherever he happened to be when the Sabbath began. Before the Sabbath began, however, one could establish a place of residence anywhere simply by placing a certain amount of food at the desired point. This "abode" then became the center from which movements were reckoned. Or, once again, there were restrictions upon cooking for the Sabbath on a Holy Day that came on a Friday. If one prepared food on Thursday and let it stand through the Sabbath, he could cook for the Sabbath on a Friday. What he did on the Friday was simply a continuation of what had begun the day before. This type of legal fiction qualified strict legalism.

In another direction it was tacitly acknowledged that the Law and the Tradition could not cover every contingency. Some rabbis taught that, in addition to observing the Law and worshiping in the temple, deeds of loving-kindness, arising out of pure compassion, were required for a fully pious life. This thought may have arisen out of the Law, but it was not strictly an interpretation of a rule.

There are other evidences, subtle though they be, of qualification of strict legalism. There was a margin of flexibility over interpretation of some laws in the disagreements of scribes. On the surface the disagreements were simply those arising from different dispositions, whether conservative or liberal, as is illustrated by Hillel and Shammai. However, they implied that the authority of the Law was not so absolute as the theory presupposed. The differences between Sadducee and Pharisee are in this category as well. If one could reach diametrically opposite conclusions about resurrection, for example, on the basis of the same Book, then the Book itself was less than absolute as revelation. The Sadducees looked upon some of the Pharisees as dangerous innovators. On the fringes of Judaism were sects whose views were not orthodox in all particulars. The Essene community at Qumran was one of them. Above all, in synagogue worship there was often an ardent and warm religious piety that had its source of inspiration elsewhere than in the legalistic premises of the priests and Pharisees.

We have previously mentioned the "people of the land." Within this context they are to be differentiated from the group known as the "associates" (*hᵃberim*), those who banded together to observe in a strict manner the laws regulating purity and tithing. They were the strict churchmen. The "people of the land" were distinguished by their laxity in observing the Law and its oral ramifications. There was often ill-feeling between the two groups. Among the "people of the land" there was, when religious sensitivity was high, a religion of the heart nurtured upon the Psalms and the Prophets. This is what became overt in John the Baptist. It was as alien to the highly technical

discussions of the rabbis as is much lay religion today. Among this
group lip service might be paid to legalism, but it was largely per-
functory. Legalistic rules were neglected in favor of a more impulsive
and intuitive religious response.

The stronghold of legalistic Judaism was Jerusalem and its environs. The further one went from the Holy City, the less strict were
legalistic practices. Galilee was thus on the perimeter of this influence.

## THE REACTIONS OF JESUS

Jesus took for granted the basic assumptions of Judaism regarding
the sovereignty of God. He began his ministry with the conviction
that he was fulfilling the faith of Israel that was rooted in these ideas.
What Jesus did was to intensify and sharpen certain features of the
conception of sovereignty, emphasizing their moral implications, out
of which grew a sharp attack upon certain other features of the conception. His attack on Jewish legalism, its premises and its implications, was devastating. He had an entirely different view as to what
it was that God demanded of his People. In this section we shall deal
briefly with the ways in which he intensified the basic assumptions,
and then elaborate more fully his ideas about God's demands upon
men.

The clue to Jesus' thought here is found in the theme of his message, namely, "the kingdom of God." We shall from this point on
translate "kingdom" by its broader connotation "reign." This is in
keeping both with the thought of Judaism and that of Jesus. According to Mark, Jesus began his public preaching with the assertion, "The
kingdom of God is at hand; repent, and believe in the gospel." Jesus
uses the term some sixty times in the first three Gospels, as against
its use some thirty-six times in the rest of the New Testament. The
figure "sixty" does not represent the total usage of the first three
Gospels. We have reached this figure by counting only once the use
of the term in three or in two sources. That is, parallel passages are
assumed to represent one saying of Jesus. The point is that, even on
this restricted basis, the term predominates in Jesus' words in the first
three Gospels.

It is not always easy to determine exactly what Jesus meant by the
expression, since he did not define it abstractly. Obviously it had

something to do with the idea of God's sovereignty as we have just
elaborated it. The background of the idea (not the term) provides us
with the key to its meaning. There were three basic facets of the conception. It expressed the fact of God's eternal rule, which was the
ground of every other aspect of it. It also denoted the expression of
God's demands upon his subjects in terms of everyday living. In addition it voiced a confident hope in God's ultimate liquidation of evil
and the fulfillment of his purposes. These three facets are clear
enough in Jesus' teaching about the reign of God.

We shall consider Jesus' teaching about the future triumph of the
reign of God in the next chapter. It belongs in both chapters, since
it expresses God's sovereignty as well as his redemptive work. However, we shall consider it primarily under the latter heading. In this
chapter we shall concern ourselves with the two other facets of the
idea. In doing so we appeal to reports of Jesus' sayings and actions that
do not explicitly contain references to the reign of God. This is necessary, since the term as such is simply a general category under which
everything that Jesus said and did belongs.

In order to simplify the treatment, we appeal to Jesus' reply to
the scribe who asked him what the greatest commandment was. The
reply of Jesus was completely in the spirit of the Judaism of his times.
After citing the Shema, asserting Judaism's basic monotheistic conviction, he said:

"You shall love the Lord your God with all your heart, and with all your
soul, and with all your mind, and with all your strength. . . . You shall
love your neighbor as yourself." There is no other commandment greater
than these.

This was a quotation from the scriptures, from Deuteronomy and
Leviticus. The ideas were fundamental to the thought of Judaism.
To that extent Jesus was but voicing the faith of Judaism, as the
scribe acknowledged. In regard to certain things in Jesus' thought
the scribe was right. Jesus and he stood on the same ground. On
the other hand, everything depended upon how one interpreted the
meaning of "love," "neighbor," and "commandment." Jesus' interpretation of these terms was radically different from that of the scribe,
and in this interpretation are to be found his distinctive emphases.

Upon these emphases we shall concentrate in the treatment to follow. The twofold commandment provides suitable headings for our thought. The first directs attention to God's sovereignty in its basic and general aspects. The second opens up the question of his demands upon men with reference to their dealings with one another.

We consider first the implications of Jesus' thought regarding the absolute love God demanded from men. As we have said, the uniqueness of Jesus lies in the intensity with which he experienced and expressed an idea fundamental to Jewish thought. As the ruler of a totalitarian regime, God demanded absolute loyalty. Everything was in God's hands. This included world history and the lives of each individual. Jesus concentrated upon the latter, even though the former was in his thought as well. Over and over he asserts or implies the supremacy of God's will. The quotation of the great commandment is but the text for many other expressions. Some of these are: "Hallowed be thy name"; "Thy kingdom come"; "Thy will be done"; "Render to Caesar the things that are Caesar's, and to God the things that are God's"; "It is written, 'You shall worship the Lord your God, and him only shall you serve' "; "Seek first his kingdom and his righteousness, and all these things shall be yours as well." Almost at random one can choose passages in the Gospels with similar import. When one is properly attuned to the reign of God he will be like a pearl merchant selling all lesser pearls in order to secure "one pearl of great value." He will count the loss of an eye or a hand cheap by comparison.

As Jesus expressed it, the sovereignty of God is made evident in the choice that is forced upon man. He cannot be neutral in the presence of God. He cannot have it both ways, serving both God and mammon. No divided loyalty is allowed. It is all or nothing. This is the nature of life as dictated by the fact that God is sovereign. Judgment is final on this basis. A man either builds a secure foundation or he does not, and he suffers the consequences of his decision. Man is forced to a decision, for or against God, that he must make. God's demand for allegiance is absolute.

The intensity with which Jesus expressed these ideas is but the counterpart of the way in which he experienced God's sovereignty in his own life. He made absolute demands upon his followers because he himself had faced the absolute demands of God upon himself and had gone all-out. The Temptation of Jesus portrays this vividly. As it stands it is probably highly interpreted by his followers, but it is thoroughly in line with everything else we know about him in the Gospels. The three alternatives he faced were to turn stones to bread, to jump from the pinnacle of the temple, and to accept from Satan authority over the world. Each in its own fashion was a subtle way of asking that God do his will rather than that he submit to God's will. Jesus saw through them and labeled them suggestions of Satan. The key to his attitude is the answer that God alone shall be served. The counterpart to this is the utterance of Jesus in Gethsemane: "Abba, Father, all things are possible to thee; remove this cup from me; yet not what I will, but what thou wilt." Relevant to this is everything that has been said in Chapter II about the nature of Jesus' authority, and also much that remains to be said in this chapter and the following one. God's sovereignty was not a theory for Jesus. It was the major fact of life, and of his own individual life in particular.

Jesus' view was thoroughly religious rather than theological. That is, it was grounded in experience rather than in thought. It was also religious rather than magical. Magic assumes that God can be used by man for his purposes, while religion assumes that man is to be used by God. Jesus gave no comfort to those who thought that God could be used to make them happy or respected or successful, or who sought his power for purposes of making an "adjustment" to their environment. To think of using God was blasphemy. God was the Sovereign, the Lord of Heaven and Earth, who demanded absolute loyalty. Man was confronted by him with a decision from the making of which he could not escape. He must serve God alone or suffer the consequences: "You shall love the Lord your God with *all* . . ."

With regard to the problem of evil, Jesus, like the New Testament as a whole, gave no philosophical answer. He would not have understood the controversy that revolves around the subject today in philosophical circles. The thought that God might in any way be "finite" would never have entered his head. His own attitude is religious. It rests upon complete faith in God's sovereignty. In some way or other God will solve the problem in his own way. His emphasis fell upon what God required of men. His views partook of the prevailing modified dualism of current thought. Two warring kingdoms stood over against each other, except that both were in origin due to God. Just how this was so was a mystery Jesus did not try to solve. He simply accepted the fact, and interpreted it with reference to God's demand upon men of complete loyalty. He saw man as the prize that was being fought for, and he asserted the importance of the kind of response that had been described. To acknowledge God as King was man's major responsibility. To assert this in word and deed was the burden of Jesus' vocation.

Jesus became more specific about this matter in his teaching relative to the Torah, or Law. As we have said, most of what he has to say arose in polemical situations. It took the form of a mighty protest against the presuppositions and the practices of the legalists. We may best see what he emphasized by taking as a heading the second commandment: "You shall love your neighbor as yourself." When we understand what he meant by that, we have got to the root of his outlook.

Undergirding his specific emphases was the foundation of thought that he had in common with his contemporaries, even when he disagreed with them. The fundamental demand of God was that of absolute obedience to his will, issuing in a life of righteousness. The problems arose over the meaning of "righteousness." We have seen the way in which the legalists interpreted it with reference to the Torah and the Oral Tradition. We have also been alerted to the ways in which Jesus challenged this, including the idea of revelation that was inherent within it. We can fulfill our purpose here, avoiding needless repetition, if we concentrate upon the implications of his thought regarding love of neighbor.

Three general ideas are involved, with several implications in each case. The commandment of love of neighbor was the only one that had absolute validity. It was the exclusive and the sole demand God placed upon men. By implication Jesus swept the detailed regulations of both the written Law and the Oral Tradition into the wastebasket. They were all supplanted by this one commandment. The people recognized the radical nature of this position when they contrasted Jesus' "authority" with the usual practices of the scribes. The scribes understood its implications too. So radical did it seem to them that they accused Jesus of being inspired by Beelzebub, the prince of demons. This also explains how his friends could believe that he was "beside himself." No agitator was more outspoken about a vested ecclesiastical interest. Jesus' views in this respect are implicit in every polemical situation in which he found himself. No matter what the issue—fasting, the Sabbath, divorce, temple worship, blasphemy, association with publicans and sinners, the Oral Tradition—his attitude is evident. Explicitly he accused the scribes of rejecting the written Law by means of their casuistry, and then he implied that even the written Law was not absolute. On the subject of divorce, for example, Jesus set one saying against another. In reality he was not appealing to the Book at all except to implement an idea that had a quite different ground of authority. A theoretical agreement with the scribes about the divine nature of the Torah collapsed in the face of what Jesus actually assumed and practiced with respect to its significance. His religion was not in any way a religion of a Book. Even his quotation of the two great commandments was not proof-texting. It was simply the most effective way to say what he knew to be true on other grounds. Thus he asserted that God's sole demand was that of love of neighbor in human relations.

The second innovation of Jesus lies in the fact that the commandment to love one's neighbor is not a rule or regulation that could be enforced by penal instrumentality. It was totally different from a rule about reaping or sewing—or going through a red light on the highway —on the Sabbath. It was an inward disposition the fruits of which only could be observed. This too implied the uselessness of a set of prescriptions designed to cover every possible contingency of human affairs. On this premise a man was not good in terms of obeying a rule. He was good if his heart was loving toward a neighbor.

In effect, this linked love of neighbor with God's love. One could love a neighbor only if he had experienced God's love in his heart. Out of that experience God's love flowed out toward a neighbor. This was not a mechanical adjustment in the machinery of thought. It was a life-giving flow of water from a spring. It was beneficial to others to the extent that its sources were sound and constant. God's love in the heart, not his will in a Book, constituted its distinguishing mark. God's love in forgiveness and in power, not human merit, was its inspiration and its power. Its motivation was the overwhelming experience of grace, not the commandment of God or the nearness of his judgment.

Jesus' view of man supported this. He was optimistic about human nature, even though he recognized man's capacity for evil. This was not an optimism based upon a false conception of man's virtue, however, but rather upon faith in God's love and power. The thing that gave dignity to man was his ability to acknowledge God's sovereignty, accept his love, and experience his power.

Related to this was Jesus' emphasis upon sincerity and receptiveness to God. Such sincerity and openness to God made repentance possible, and out of that arose in man awareness of what God was doing for him, in him, and through him.

Thus Jesus drove home the truth that right conduct issues from a right disposition infused with the love of God. The fruit of the tree is determined by its nature in this sense. "From within, out of the heart of man, come evil thoughts" and good thoughts, and their fruits in conduct defile him or exalt him. Ritual regulations cannot make a man pure in heart, which is the crucial matter. If one wishes to observe the sacred laws about murder and adultery, which Jesus supported, he must cleanse his heart of anger and lust. These acts begin in imagination. Only the positive power of love, love like that of God's love, can prevent wrong thinking which issues inevitably in actions harmful to one's neighbor. So intense is Jesus in his teaching on this point that he equates the thought with the deed. To think murder is to kill and to imagine adultery is to perform the act. God does condemn the wrong thought just as much in this respect as he does insincerity in fasting, prayer, and almsgiving. The point, however, is that right conduct requires right thinking. Or, it requires a heart at one with God's love for man.

It might seem that Jesus was very unrealistic about the nature and the importance of law in the light of this emphasis. However, this is to ask more of his teaching than he intended. He did not face the question of the need of a legal structure in an organized society. He apparently confined himself to emphasizing that which he felt needed emphasis under the specific conditions of his day that legalism produced. His emphasis was on inner motive and disposition because this was neglected by those whom he attacked. In the face of a system that interpreted goodness in terms of conformity to endless rules, and in so doing embodied all the faults of an extreme legalism, he attempted to redress the balance. He did it with an exaggerated and a seemingly one-sided stress upon inner conditions, but he did so because that

was what the situation required. He was not teaching in a vacuum
or attempting to set forth systematically a complete theory of ethics.
The implications of his thought permit us to assert that he would have
recognized any means by which human societies might be beneficently
regulated for the common good. We know that laws serve that purpose. Traffic regulations but typify it. That Jesus is silent on the question does not warrant the conclusion that he was impractical. He
stressed what he did because that was what was required in his circumstances. In that sense he was no more one-sided than the ancient
prophets upon whose shoulders he stood. The prophets were impractical too in the sense that Jesus was. They placed their finger upon
the heart of Israel's disease without trying to answer every question of
an ethical nature.

The third facet of Jesus' thought relative to love of neighbor is the
way in which he redefined "neighbor" with reference to prevailing
ideas of what it meant. In this respect he took seriously the full implications of ethical monotheism. There was a tendency, having a long
history, to equate "neighbor" with "fellow Israelite." This was not
universally so, but it was implied in the legalistic premises. The purpose of the legalistic procedure was to effect a means of keeping the
People pure, separated from contamination by outside influences.
The term "Pharisee" means "separated," and the party arose in the
first place out of a concern to apply the Law strictly to the end of
Israel's purity. The most enlightened social legislation of the Old
Testament in Deuteronomy distinguished between native Israelite
and resident alien, and, while protecting the latter in some ways, never
gave him the privileges of full citizenship. Jesus for all practical purposes abolished any distinctions whatsoever. He viewed man as such
before God without concern for his nationality or race or sex or anything else. He confined his labors to his own people, generally speaking, but the implication of his outlook was universalistic in the extreme.

This is evident in many ways in his teaching and his practice. It
is the implication of his concern for the individual as a soul to be
saved rather than with social legislation. We recall his sayings about
rich men in this connection, and there are others. An intense individualism is universalistic in its effects. When one sees the individual
in his essential characteristics as one created in the image of God, the

accidental characteristics of nationality, race, sex, social status recede
into the background. One is only secondarily Israelite, Samaritan,
Gentile. Primarily he is man. The Parable of the Good Samaritan
implies much in this respect. That Jesus should employ a Samaritan
as an example of neighborliness is in itself almost as significant as the
point of the parable. It is like a died-in-the-wool segregationist using
a Negro as an example, or like a right-wing Republican using a Communist. The point of the parable answers Jesus' question, "Which of
these three, do you think, proved neighbor to the man who fell among
robbers?" The Samaritan, of course, in contrast to the representatives
of official piety. Why? Because he understood the true meaning of
"neighbor." It was defined by human need, not by rules designed to
separate a man from his neighbor on the basis of nationality or ceremonial purity. That the Sabbath is made for man teaches the same
lesson as does the claim that the temple is "a house of prayer for all
nations."

Jesus is most explicit on this point in what he says directly about
love of enemy. This includes a readiness to forgive and a magnanimity
that elevates the relationship above the realm of legal procedures. The
key to the whole is in the saying "Pray for those who persecute you."
That means to take the issue into the presence of God and seek his
guidance. Since God is infinitely forgiving and infinitely merciful,
one cannot treat his enemy in any other way, if he is completely dedicated to God. The exhortation to turn the other cheek is not a rule
for conduct. It is a figurative way of saying that one does not deal
with anyone else in terms of what is done to him. The standard is
quite different. One sets every neighbor before God. His motivation
in dealing with him is always the same. He seeks his welfare in an
unselfish manner. If the neighbor is an enemy, this requires sur-
mounting the temptation to vindictiveness and getting even. The
basic motivation and efforts to implement it are the same in the case
of enemy and friend.

Jesus has been accused of being impractical in this respect, but,
once again, this is due to asking of him more than he intended. He
was not working out in detail all the perplexing questions that arise
in this connection. He gives no consideration to the problem of what
to do when the real choice is, as it usually is, between evils rather
than between black and white. His teaching was conditioned by a

situation in which "neighbor" was defined exclusively and in which the responsibility of loving the alien or the foreigner was not always included in the general prescription. Against that he set his face, without examining all its implications. That this was true of God's character and, by implication, of human conduct pleasing to him— that was his concern. The basic attitude, as it was grounded in a vital experience with God the Father, was what he stressed. It is not correct to say that he was not trying to be practical, but true. He was concerned with the practicalities of daily living, but in terms of its foundation. Thus he stated what God required in absolute terms, leaving to the imagination and the ingenuity of men its specific application in their circumstances. Because God's love was absolute he had to require an absolute performance of men.

Jesus' own example reinforces his teaching. We have already observed that in accepting death on a cross he did it for his enemies as well as for his friends. It was the ultimate expression of his love, to die for his enemies rather than oppose them with a sword. His seeking out of the outcasts in his society, those who to strict legalists were enemies, was, besides the acceptance of the cross, the chief way in which Jesus embodied this love. References that indicate sympathy with outsiders—a Roman centurion, a Syrophoenician woman, a Samaritan—suggest the breadth of his outlook. All men were potential members of God's family. Deeper than human ties of any sort, whether of family or nation, were those that bound all men to the sovereign God who was a God of absolute and infinite love. To exclude enemies from this circle would have been to deny its true nature. The love he taught was much more aggressive and much more inclusive. It was in nature like that of Edwin Markham's thought:

> He drew a circle which shut me out,
> Heretic, rebel, a thing to flout.
> But love and I had the wit to win.
> We drew a circle which took him in.

This was not a sentimental quality. Jesus was wise enough to know that nothing so disrupted the heart of man and the society in which he lived as hatred. He might well, had he known them, have quoted the words of W. B. Yeats' "A Prayer for My Daughter":

My mind, because the minds that I have loved,
The sort of beauty that I have approved,
Prosper but little, has dried up of late,
Yet knows that to be choked with hate
May well be of all evil chances chief.
If there's no hatred in a mind
Assault and battery of the wind
Can never tear the linnet from the leaf.

Nothing in history has made the truth of that so emphatic as Jesus' own conduct and its sequel.

It remains only to point out certain implications of Jesus' approach to questions of conduct pleasing to God. They represent the views of any creative spirit in the presence of legalism, but the character of Jesus gives them emphatic dynamic. Jesus stated God's demands in absolute terms, even though he had practical situations in mind. He brought vertical vision to bear upon the horizontal situation. He was more concerned with the right and wrong of things than with whether he stood to right or left of the center of popular opinion. The latter could not be right unless the former was. He offered directions, as it were, with reference to aims and goals and basic values rather than with reference to practical schemes by means of which to implement them. He dealt with courtesy, not rules of etiquette.

This fundamental distinction placed upon men the obligation to use their minds in working out detailed application of the basic values. Great ingenuity and imagination were required, ever alert and ever ready to deal with new contingencies. Life was not like a detective story with a cut-and-dried solution. Because of unforeseen factors the plot of life was not always soluble, and it might be changed at any moment. In practical affairs one had to contend with the possible, which was seldom the ideal, and be wise in compromise. The effects of a given course of conduct, as well as its motivation, had to be considered, and the course changed accordingly. This placed upon men a tremendous responsibility. It is no wonder that most men prefer an authoritarian system that tells them what to do rather than "The Protestant Principle" that stems from Jesus.

Jesus called for aggressive and positive action in conduct. Silence in the face of the demand to speak out was itself sin. To run into the law for being ahead of the times was in a very different category from criminal action against society. Sins of omission were equally condemned with sins of commission. In the face of injustice, in large or small dimensions, the spirit of Jesus was that of Louis Untermeyer:

> Ever insurgent let me be,
> Make me more daring than devout.

The ability to grow was also implied. Jesus stressed humility at the same time that he set perfection as the goal. He said that one was always unworthy as compared with God's goodness but that he could advance toward the ideal. Conversion is but a beginning. It opens the door and sets one in a position to develop. Paul understood this when he said, "Forgetting the things which are behind, I press on. . . ." In one respect growth rested upon an absolute. This applies as well to the problem of compromise in practical situations. Love of neighbor, inflaming motivation and its implementation, should never be compromised. One might make mistakes in applying love, but love itself was the absolute requirement. Even then, one grows in grace.

Finally, Jesus' basic views implied an inclusive coverage of situations of which the legal system could not boast. It was a different kind of coverage. It did not establish minute rules for every conceivable situation. Instead it brought to bear upon every issue right motivation and indications for implementation that never changed. As we have seen, intelligence and imagination were required to find out what this meant, but the basic requirements were given. Although Jesus gave no attention to the larger social extension of his basic ideas, such an extension is implicit in his outlook. Not only is every situation covered, but every conceivable situation is of necessity included by love. The great judgment scene asserts that the criterion of judgment is humanitarian service: visiting the imprisoned, feeding the hungry, clothing the naked. Jesus did not say that this applied to its extension in foreign-aid programs or social-security plans, but the implication is there. The love that Jesus taught and embodied leaves no area of human need out of account. This love is "broader than the measure of man's mind" in more ways than one.

In this way Jesus reacted to the idea of the sovereignty of God in his native Judaism. Establishing himself firmly upon the ground of Israel's faith, he rebelled against practices that to him curtailed and misrepresented its true genius. In so doing he became the great insurgent, the radical agitator against the *status quo*. Is it any wonder that he was finally eliminated by those in power?

# 5

## GOD THE REDEEMER

✤✤✤✤✤✤✤ That God had a redemptive purpose in the thought of Judaism and of Jesus has already been indicated in various ways. As Creator and as Sovereign all of his activity was beneficent in intention and in implementation. Two aspects of this general fact call for special attention, however, in this chapter: God's way of dealing with sin and his plans for the future.

### THE THOUGHT OF JUDAISM

Our first concern is with the question of sin and forgiveness. We have already been made aware of the nature of sin as disobedience to God's revealed will, both ceremonially and ethically considered. We have also noted the emphasis upon the individual. At least in the thought of the more prophetically-minded priests and scribes the individual was responsible to God for his thought and conduct. There lingered, to be sure, the idea that when the fathers ate sour grapes the teeth of their children were set on edge, but there was no doctrine of original sin. The sense of sin was acutely alive in Jesus' time. Despite apocalyptic forecasts of judgment designed to justify God to man in the face of the problem of evil, the idea of retribution would not let him believe that he was guiltless before God. Among the humble, more affected by prophetic than by legalistic thought, the question of God's way of dealing with sin was especially sharp. But it was one that the whole People faced.

Judaism taught the forgiveness of God as his way of reconciling man to himself. The condition of receiving forgiveness was repentance. God's offer of forgiveness was a sheer act of grace on his part. It was free and abundant, but it was conditioned by man's sincere repentance. This meant a genuine facing in the opposite direction, complete self-surrender, the return of a life to its true center. This was Jewish thought at its best. In certain circles meritorious works were considered almost a substitute for moral renewal, as though man could achieve the right to salvation. Only later, however, in Hellenistic Judaism, did the idea arise that the righteous dead contributed to the removal of the stain of sin. This question was not influenced by the merits of the ancient patriarchs. They may have predisposed God to be gracious to Israel in the days of its Election, but that was as far as it went. It could not alter the conditions of the present.

With regard to what a man must do in order to secure remission of his sin, ritual and ethical elements were both involved. The following quotation is typical of certain ritualistic conditions:

A great general rule have they laid down concerning the Sabbath: whosoever, forgetful of the principle of the Sabbath, committed many acts of work on many Sabbaths, is liable only to one sin offering; but if, mindful of the principle of the Sabbath, he yet committed many acts of work on many Sabbaths, he is liable for every Sabbath which he profaned. If he knew that it was the Sabbath and he yet committed many acts of work on many Sabbaths, he is liable for every main class of work which he performed; if he committed many acts of work of one main class, he is liable only to one sin offering.

The quotation implies the expectation that a man might be careless, even willful.

The distinction between acts committed knowingly and in ignorance is also evident in the general theory of atonement (at-one-ment) for sins committed against one's fellow man. Ethical and ritualistic elements are both present. Atonement must be made both to God and man for three classes of sin. The first is sin committed unconsciously and unintentionally. The annual Day of Atonement provided for that. On that day the high priest entered the Holy of Holies in the temple, representing the People, to receive God's forgiveness. The second class was sin committed consciously and intentionally against a neighbor. For this, confession, restoration, and reparation were required. The third class was a particularly flagrant instance of the second class, "sins of a high hand." There was no solution of this except the completely unmerited mercy of God. In regard to no class of sin, however, was forgiveness unavailing, provided that sincere repentance was forthcoming. The only unforgivable sin was the refusal to accept the gift of grace God freely offered. It was conceivable that a man might be so obstinate or so steeped in self-love that he literally could not repent.

Involved in this whole question was much speculation in Jesus' day about life after death. This rightly forms a transition to the next section dealing with the future hope. It is relevant here to the extent that the question of forgiveness was closely tied in with that of future rewards and punishments in apocalyptic thought.

Some understanding of Hebrew anthropology and psychology is required to make intelligible the nature of Jewish thought about the destiny of the individual. Man was conceived as composed of a body and an inner vital principle. God had infused the "breath of life" (spirit or pneuma) into man at the time of the Creation. Neither element could exist without the other. Man was always viewed in his wholeness or entirety as an indissoluble union of these elements. The body was simply the outward manifestation of the soul or life. Various terms were used to designate the whole and its parts, but we need not go into them. The crucial point can be made without doing that: life after death could only be pictured by the Jewish mind in terms of some form of bodily existence. He did not hold with the Hellenists (or moderns) that an immortal soul left the frail body behind at death. Paul's "spiritual body" in I Corinthians was thoroughly Jewish. It might not be of flesh and blood, but it was still a body.

During the centuries prior to the time of Jesus there was no genuine belief among the Hebrews in the survival of the individual after death. It is not Old Testament doctrine. There was a belief among some in Sheol as the land of the dead, but it was a shadowy realm

with which God had nothing to do. The Sadducees still championed
that view in Jesus' time. On that premise the only solution of the
problem of death, caused by Adam's error, was to live as long as possible. This explains why a long and happy life was of such importance,
and why the problem of evil was so acute to a man like Job. The
Hebrew genius was conditioned to equate happiness on earth with
righteousness pleasing to God rather than in terms of "eat, drink, and
be merry, for tomorrow we die." But in each case death was final and
this life was all one had.

Various influences, among them Persian thought, led to speculation on the part of the Pharisees about a future destiny for the individual beyond death. The result was the doctrine of resurrection. The
essential motive in achieving this result was the growing conviction
that God would provide compensation for the righteous individual
who, like Job, had been mistreated or who had undeservedly suffered
on earth. There was, however, no consistency in regard to details
about this future life among those who speculated. In some thought
Sheol developed from an unpleasant place under the earth into the
place or condition in which the righteous would enjoy eternal life.
It was not agreed whether this would be on earth or someplace else.
In the mind of others Sheol was the place or condition of punishment.
Gehenna also served this purpose. On the assumption that the
righteous would be resurrected, there was no agreement as to whether
they would rise alone, or, if so, when: immediately at death or after
an interim period. About the exact circumstances of the fate of
unrepentant sinners there was just as much disagreement. Ideas of
their torment jostled those who held that they would be extinguished.
The only general agreement was that the body of the individual would
rise in some renewed form. The Essenes deviated somewhat from this.
They were influenced by Hellenistic assumptions regarding the distinction between body and soul. The Sadducees, as we have said,
repudiated the idea of resurrection altogether. The great majority of
the people followed the Pharisees. They accepted its initial assumption at least to the effect that, since God did not always reward goodness in this life, he must do it in another. In no other way could his
justice and his mercy be sustained in thought.

This leads directly into the question of the future hope of Judaistic
thought in its broader dimensions. The scholars employ a technical

term by means of which to designate this future hope: eschatology. *Eschatos* means "last" or "final," so that "eschatology" is the science, the study, the doctrine, of the last things. In our context it deals with questions pertinent to the goal that God had set for history in the act of creation. The subject belongs properly under the heading of God the Redeemer because it is an expression of faith in his redemptive activity, even though his creatorship and sovereignty are inextricably intertwined with it.

We may remind ourselves that Hebrew thought about the future had one consistent presupposition at all times: history was moving under God's guidance toward a target. It was not a roulette wheel endlessly circling and getting nowhere. Nor was it an endless existence. This was moral in tone. God's justice must at some time assert itself unequivocally and with finality, destroying all evil and all rebellion against his will. All history was pictured with reference to the conflict between good and evil. Since God was in control of the whole process, the scales had to be balanced. When God was ready to act, this would come to pass.

This was the basic presupposition of the Hebrew philosophy of history at all times. However, it was differently conceived at different times. By considering the foundation laid by prophetic thought we shall be in a position to understand the currents of thought that were most alive in Jesus' day. The fundamental premise of the prophets was that God would be true to his Covenant. Their convictions about the future were religiously oriented. That is, their predictions about the future grew out of their sensitivity to God's moral nature rather than from an estimate of the political probabilities. They were, to be sure, wise in foreign politics. They knew what the great empires in the Tigris-Euphrates and the Nile River valleys were doing. Much of what they had to say concerned the conquest of the nation by these foreign foes. But they were not politicians who put a dampened finger into the wind of popular sentiment before making pronouncements. It was "the false prophet" who did this in an effort to please the rulers and the populace. The true prophet said what God told him to say, whether his message was popular or not. He was more concerned to be true to his vision of God than to be "practical."

Their views of the future were conditioned by the fact that as yet no doctrine of a life beyond the grave had come into being. God's new day following his judgment upon the nation was earth-bound. Since the future developed "continuously out of the present," good and evil bearing their own fruit, this had to be the way they thought. The prophets did not speculate unduly about the nature of this future condition beyond the central thought that God's judgment would be strictly ethical in nature.

By the time of Jesus the prophetic view had been considerably modified. There were two main types of thought. They overlapped somewhat in certain respects, yet each possessed distinguishing characteristics of its own. One was nationalistic eschatology, or messianism. It was grounded in the theocratic idea of God as King, and it held that this idea would be fulfilled in terms of the exaltation of the nation to its destined place in the sun. The tarnished political glory of God's People would be realized through God's act. A messiah like David would arise from among men to act for God in bringing this to pass. The Romans would be driven out, and in the ensuing judgment all the Gentiles would be punished. If the fate of the Gentiles was not always so strictly understood, the predominant bias was very nationalistic in tone.

The other type of thought may be called cosmic or apocalyptic eschatology. It is represented by such writings as Daniel, Enoch, IV Ezra, and (in the New Testament) the Revelation of John. It flourished for a period of three hundred years from approximately 200 B.C. to A.D. 100. It was "cosmic" in the sense that, in contrast to the prophetic view, it was not earth-bound. It assumed that there were two ages, the present and the future. The future it foresaw was "essentially discontinuous with the present." Judgment would not be simply the reaping in this life of what had been sown. It would be a revolutionary breaking off of the historical process, a leap to a new level of existence. Normal history would end and a "new heaven and a new earth" would be created by God's act. Two cosmic kingdoms were at war, one being that of God and the other that of Satan. Since Satan existed only because God permitted him to, he and his battalions of evil angels would be destroyed when the great day came.

The word "apocalyptic" is vital to the understanding of this outlook. The noun "apocalypse" means "revelation" or "unveiling." The Revelation of John, for example, is the Apocalypse of John. In the nature of the case the apocalyptic seer believed that he was divinely endowed to penetrate the veil between this earth and the cosmic regions. Thus his writing described what things were like in heaven and what the future would be. Speculation about every facet of this subject went to fantastic lengths among the self-styled apocalyptists. The prophet made predictions on the basis of what he thought God was saying with reference to current events. The apocalyptist, however, had his head above the clouds in an area the prophets could not even have imagined as existing.

This type of thought had other characteristics as well, which we shall outline very briefly. We shall simply indicate them here, leaving further elaboration until we deal with the way in which Jesus related himself to this outlook. It was held that the final events were moving to their culmination on a predetermined schedule. God had set the date for history to end, and he alone knew its exact moment. The apocalyptists speculated as to when it would come, being convinced that it would be soon and that they could discern the time. They believed that certain signs of the End would herald its approach. These signs were called the Messianic Woes. Great distress in the form of political and military oppression or of supernatural portents in nature, or a combination of both, would be the sure sign that the End was at hand. Then would come the judgment, separating the sheep and the goats. What has been said previously about the subject of resurrection applies at this point. The faithful would receive their reward; the sinners would be punished or exterminated. Narrow nationalistic prejudices mingled with more ethical considerations in picturing the criterion of judgment. Among some it was believed that an interim period would exist between God's victory over Satan and the final End. The length of time was set forth in symbolical numbers (400 or 1,000 years) designating an indefinite period. The purpose of this interval was to give the martyrs a special reward before all the other righteous people were resurrected. After that, the arrow of God's purpose would reach its target finally and irrevocably.

Corresponding to the idea of Davidic messiahship, apocalypticism often assumed that God would be assisted by a heavenly man (Son of man). Speculation about such a figure was rife in Jesus' day. The important point is that he was envisaged as a preexistent being coming from heaven rather than as a person who would, like the Son of

David, arise from among men. Other thinkers believed that God would act alone in the final events, without assistance beyond battalions of angels. Thus apocalyptic thought contributed to the growth of the doctrine of angels.

It remains only to mention the symbolism by means of which apocalypticism expressed its ideas. Two major reasons caused apocalyptists to say what they had to say in a coded message. One was because they were writing subversive literature. Because their message usually was directed against the government, they did not want it understood by the officials. The other reason was simply the fact that they had a flair for this particular kind of expression. As the poet has his own way of saying things, so the apocalyptist. In other words, the apocalyptist was an apocalyptist just because he was. His way of expressing himself about the future was the way he felt about it.

An example of the symbolism employed can be more useful than much abstract description. In Daniel 7 we are told of a vision the writer had. In the vision he saw four great beasts coming up from the sea:

The first was like a lion and had eagles' wings. Then as I looked its wings were plucked off, and it was lifted up from the ground and made to stand upon two feet like a man; and the mind of a man was given to it.

The second beast was like a bear with three ribs in his mouth. The third was like a leopard with four wings and four heads. The fourth was not compared to an animal, but it had great iron teeth with which it destroyed things and then trampled upon the residue. What distinguished it from the others, however, was that it had ten horns. Among these horns a smaller one grew in which were "eyes like the eyes of a man, and a mouth speaking great things." This horn plucked up three of the first horns by the roots. Eventually the beast is slain, his body destroyed and burned. The other three beasts remain for "a season and a time." In IV Ezra 11 an eagle comes up from the sea, with twelve wings and three heads, and eight antiwings. Eventually the eagle is destroyed by a lion. The Revelation of John has a beast coming up out of the sea having ten horns and seven heads, one of the heads bearing a scar. A second beast rises out of the earth and exercises the authority of the first beast. It has two horns. Both beasts serve the dragon. The number 666 is said to be the number of the first beast.

Apparently in each case the beast is a symbol of the government in power at the time. For Daniel in the second century B.C. it is Syria to the north. For IV Ezra and the Revelation to John, both written later in the first century after Christ, it is Rome. The horns of the beasts or the heads of the eagle stand for individual rulers. The head bearing a scar in the Revelation of John probably means Nero. It was widely believed that he was not really dead, but residing with the Parthians to the east from whence he would return to defeat his enemies in Rome. The lion who destroys the eagle in IV Ezra, corresponding to other figures in different apocalypses, is the messiah who defeats the earthly powers that are in rebellion against God. The number 666 signifies the use of numerals as symbols. In this case the combination of three sixes means the depth of degradation. Ingenious schemes are worked out to decipher this numeral with reference to a particular Roman emperor. It may be that it stands for Nero, but whether it does or not, it symbolizes his evil character. Seven (or twelve) is the symbol of completeness or perfection. Since six is less than seven it stands for imperfection, and a combination of three such numerals adds to the degree of imperfection or evil.

This is but a sample of apocalyptic symbolism. It takes various figures that are not to be literally envisaged, and uses them to signify related ideas. The iron teeth of the beast, for instance, symbolize the persecuting power of a ruler hostile to Judaism. The eagle's wings spread out over the earth symbolize Rome's conquests. Only as one reads the apocalypses can he fully appreciate this weird manner of expression. Most of these symbols are derived from earlier literature, but the seer claims to have seen them in a vision. It is to his way of thinking a type of "special revelation" he is privileged to see and understand. By this means he expresses his faith in God's ultimate triumph over evil. It is not only a message about the future but also one about the present. He informs his readers that, although the clouds of oppression obscure it for the moment, God really is in his heaven steadfastly supporting his People.

The common denominator in all these forms of the future hope was the sense of expectancy that convictions about God's mercy and justice led them to hold in the face of the problem of evil. Expectancy of events soon to come to pass was very much alive in Jesus' day. Especially in Galilee the flame must have burned brightly, although it was not confined to that locality. The Qumran community in the Dead Sea wilderness was acutely expectant with an apocalyptic perspective. They had retired to the desert in order to discipline themselves for the anticipated Holy War that would herald the End. This was the climate in which John the Baptist appeared and to which he contributed. "The kingdom of heaven is at hand," he said. It will bring a mightier one than himself who will come with a judgment of fire. Therefore, "repent!"

## THE REACTIONS OF JESUS

The topics to be treated here follow naturally from the preceding section. The first is the question of sin and of how God deals with it. Jesus assumed the fundamental views of Judaism regarding the nature of sin. It was disobedience to God, and it was a matter of individual decision. In a radical manner Jesus made the individual the focal point of his message. Unlike the ancient prophets, he did not address the nation as such. Certain sayings and parables do apply to groups, especially the Jewish leaders, but this does not change his emphasis upon the responsibility of the individual within the group. In all this, except for the radical way in which he stressed some things, he was not very different from his contemporaries.

Where Jesus differed from them, with regard to the nature of sin, was in the emphasis he placed upon its moral aspects. Except to relegate them to a subordinate status, he gave no attention at all to ritual matters. He isolated the moral elements and said that they alone really mattered. This did not mean that he was opposed to ceremonial practices such as circumcision or fasting or the temple sacrifices. He attended synagogue services and worshiped in the temple. All this was essentially irrelevant, however, to the question of sin. Sin was the failure to obey God's commandment to love, and virtue was to love. Ritual practices had nothing to do with that. Before one could worship in Jesus' sense of the term, one's heart must be pure. The distinguishing mark of the obedience God demanded was love of enemy: "If you love those who love you, what reward have you?" Anyone could do that. It proved nothing, and ceremonial piety proved less. That is to say, Jesus' radical attitude toward Jewish legalism extended inevitably into the area of the definition of sin. The whole Torah was worthy of observance to the extent that it inculcated a genuine love. The rest did not really matter.

The emphasis of Jesus fell upon the infinite mercy of God in dealing with sinners. The idea was not new with him, except in two ways. There was first an extravagance about the way in which he portrayed it. His most typical saying in this respect was that in which he compared God's attitude with the loving parent, and then in degree placed God in a class by himself: "If you, then, who are evil, know how to give good gifts to your children, how much more will the heavenly Father give the Holy Spirit [or good things] to those who ask him?" The best that human beings are is but a flashlight on a dark night as compared with the mighty beacon of God's light. God's providential care and concern for men surpass the ability of the human mind to comprehend. The same extravagant quality attaches to God's mercy in dealing with sinners.

Consider other typical expressions of Jesus' convictions about this. The Parable of the Prodigal Son comes immediately to mind. The father runs to meet the returning son. All considerations of retribution are swallowed up in the exhilaration over the fact that the lost has been found. The twin Parables of the Lost Sheep and the Lost Coin are in the same spirit. That God's forgiveness has been effective produces acclaim in heaven itself. In another parable the debts of two men, one large and one small, are forgiven, and in still another parable a debtor is released from paying the sum of $10,000,000. The extravagant nature of God's forgiveness is thus set forth, as it is also in Jesus' reply to Peter's question about the number of times he should forgive his neighbor. To suggest seven times as the limit was generous, but Jesus lifted the question out of the realm of mathematics altogether. "Seventy times seven" had nothing to do with bookkeeping. It was equivalent to infinite and limitless forgiveness. This indicated Jesus' view of God's mercy. Man might refuse to accept it, but that would not change God's spirit. His mercy extended to everyone, even to those who opposed his rule. The Jerusalem over which he wept, and upon which judgment was passed, was as eligible for forgiveness as was Peter. Those who crucified Jesus without knowing what they were doing were not outside the pale.

The Parable of the Prodigal Son suggests another aspect of this question. It implies a connection between Jesus' convictions about God's mercy and his own actions in seeking out the tax collectors and sinners. In its original setting the parable was probably a polemical instrument directed against the exclusiveness of those whom the older brother typified. Their premise was that forgiveness had to be earned. It had to be deserved. Jesus did not neglect the conditions of receiving forgiveness, as we shall see. For the moment it is important to concentrate upon the assumption that forgiveness was itself an instrument of producing repentance. Paul became a new creature out of the wonder at One who would give his only Son for him before he deserved it. In the same vein Jesus challenged his opponents with the thought that God sought men in order to redeem them. In seeking out the tax collectors and sinners, Jesus was exemplifying God's method of treating unworthy men. Jesus thus dramatized the fact of God's infinite mercy, but he was not play-acting. This came from the heart. It came from a vivid and intense awareness of what God was like. In reverse, his own sympathy may well have convinced him that God must be as forgiving as he was, but "how much more" so!

The extravagance of Jesus' portrayal of God's forgiving mercy is also suggested by the fact that only in passing does he refer to God's attributes of transcendence and majesty. God was Creator and Sovereign. There was no question about that. However, Jesus' stress fell upon his spiritual and moral quality. He implied that God's glory was not primarily to be observed in nature, in holiness of an amoral kind, or even in attributes of omniscience and omnipotence. It was to be seen in his infinite love as the nucleus of his ethical character. As Jesus gave more attention to his own work of love than to definitions of his status, so he emphasized God's ethical quality. Such a God would be little impressed by flattery with regard to his creatorship, especially in ceremonial form. Because of the importance of his own love for his creatures, the only kind of worship he could really accept would be that of love returned. This would indeed be to glorify him.

In all this, Jesus did not neglect the point the older brother in the parable was trying to make, namely, that man had an obligation to God. Jesus did not neglect the quality of justice in God's nature.

God's offer of forgiveness was infinite, and nothing could change it, but man did have to do something about it. What he had to do was, according to Jesus, exactly what normative Judaism said: repent! The call to repentance rings throughout the sayings of Jesus. The wayward son was received with joyous forgiveness, but before this could happen he had to come to himself. The joy in heaven over the lost sheep that was found was due to the repentant spirit of the person it symbolized. The man who was forgiven a debt of $10,000,000 sacrificed the offer because he failed to appreciate it and meet its conditions. The tax collector in the temple had only one advantage over the proud Pharisee: he was humbly repentant. The pearl of great price, like a symphony, had to be appreciated before its worth was known. Failure to repent brought severity in judgment. If Jesus' generation failed in this respect in the face of "something greater than Jonah," it would reap the whirlwind. Like certain Galileans persecuted by the Roman procurator, like those crushed by the tower of Siloam, Jesus' listeners would perish if they did not repent. These but typify Jesus' consistent demand.

Repentance was implied in other ways of appealing for a response. A receptive spirit was one of these ways. The unsound eye that darkened understanding and could not read the signs of the times closed the door to God's benefits. Blasphemy against the Holy Spirit, the only unforgivable sin, was of this nature. A man might be so steeped in self-interest that he lost the ability to recognize his need of forgiveness, and thus could not receive it. Over against this was the seeing eye, the hearing ear. At root it was purity of heart, hungering and thirsting after righteousness, humility. It was the childlike capacity of eagerly grasping for the thing most desired, or the ability to grow. It was the insight that enabled one to understand the deeper level of Jesus' parables. On the surface a parable was simply an interesting story. So David understood Nathan's story of the man whose one lamb had been taken by another with many lambs in his own fold. David was furious with the man until Nathan replied, "But you are the man!" David needed insight in order to see that he was the man who, in taking Bathsheba from Uriah, had committed this foul deed. So with the parables of Jesus. One needed a receptive spirit in order to get the religious or moral point. This was an aspect of repentance, or perhaps its precondition. Jane Addams portrayed the meaning

of this vividly in "There Is a River." A certain person went in search
of the River of God. Returning from the futile quest for it in heaven,
he was greeted with these words:

> "O, Fool, you have travelled far to find
> What you've crossed over time and again;
> For the River of God is in Halstead Street
> And is running black with men."

> "Then maybe Chicago's the City of God?"
> Said I. "Perhaps," said he;
> "For to find that City you need no wings
> To fly, but eyes to see. . . ."

Faith was an ingredient of repentance. This was in part perhaps
the confidence in the healer required for the cure of the patient. It
was more the quality that enabled a man to release his spiritual resources in the face of any contingency. If man had faith no greater
than the smallest of seeds, Jesus said, he could upend a mountain.
That is, no problem was too great for a man empowered with God's
might. Jesus' teaching about prayer accords with this. The condition
of prayer was "Thy will be done," which implied confidence in God
enough to obey him. Absolute sincerity was a prerequisite, acknowl-
edging God as Sovereign. Faith was at the root of this as of the ability
to accept forgiveness.

Jesus was sharply distinguished from the rabbis and scribes by
calling for personal allegiance as a condition of salvation. The Parable of the Houses typifies this. One house is set upon rock, the other
upon sand, and the storm will test the foundation. If one wants security, he must accept Jesus' words and do them. What has previously
been said about the nature of Jesus' authority must guide us here. His
subject, which was God, was more important than himself. It was
more important than explaining exactly who he was. That is, Jesus
called men to God. In calling men to himself he was simply doing
what many do who are identified with their cause. Personal allegiance
to Jesus was thus but another way of describing the repentant spirit.

Looking back, we observe in Jesus' thought the combination of
mercy and justice in his view of God. This was not new, but in the
emphatic way in which Jesus brought out their meaning there was

an unusual element. He underlined what were staples in the faith of Judaism. There is a unique feature in Jesus' teaching, however, that goes beyond the fact of emphasis or extravagant statement. He made repentance the sole condition of forgiveness. He gave no place at all to the type of ritualistic atonement we have seen to be mixed up with ethical considerations in Jewish thinking. He was completely and consistently prophetic in spirit. His emphasis was exclusively moral, almost brutally so. Nothing could in any way whatsoever qualify strict moral repentance. There was no "good work" that man could perform as a substitute for ethical repentance or that he could place alongside it to strengthen it. The extra fasts and tithes of the Pharisee in the temple gave him no advantage over the publican. Abundant gifts to the temple out of superabundance were less significant than the widow's pittance without genuine humility before God in ethical terms. Ritual means of expiating sins were for all practical purposes useless. They might symbolize a changed heart, but they could not change it. By themselves they could not make things right between man and God. Long penitential prayers were in the same category. The simplicity and the directness of the Lord's Prayer remind us of that, as well as Jesus' words about insincere prayer.

No merit of man could in any way solve the problem of his sin. Man was absolutely naked before God. He was as naked as the following poem suggests:

> Why am I so afraid
> To let God speak?
> He will want me to discard
> All rubbish from my life,
> The dear, accumulated rubbish
> That I love so much.
> He will clean me out,
> Down to the bare essentials of my being.
> I am afraid,
> Afraid of the nakedness that I will feel.

Fear, among other things, prompted Jesus' contemporaries to exalt themselves, their achievements, and their good works. They would win God's favor thereby, they thought. To Jesus this was all "rubbish." To be honest enough to stand naked before God and to trust his love—this was to repent. Thus cleansed of pride and egoism and self-love, God's love would have a chance to work even greater miracles of grace.

One additional point must be considered here. It is the idea in Jesus' sayings that in order to experience God's mercy one must himself possess a forgiving spirit. The Parable of the Unmerciful Servant highlights this. A debt of $10,000,000 was canceled, but the one to whom this favor was extended turned around to demand of his debtors repayment of sums that were by comparison negligible. He did not forgive as he had been forgiven. Thus the original offer was withdrawn. The question is how one gets a forgiving spirit. The answer of Jesus, it would seem, is that one gets it from experiencing God's forgiveness. Knowing himself forgiven, man's gratitude takes the form of a reproduction of God's mercy. Repentance manifests its reality and genuineness in this quality. Ability to forgive, eagerness, even, is the sign of the spirit that has received God's forgiveness. Everything about Jesus' thought leads us to see in this, not a bargain between God and man—a tit-for-tat arrangement—but a dynamic experience. The Parable of the Unmerciful Servant was a way of saying that the servant who had been forgiven was not truly repentant nor was he grateful for the favor of his employer. Thus his debt could not be forgiven. If he had been truly repentant in Jesus' sense of that term, he would also have forgiven his debtors.

We turn now to the subject of the future hope (eschatology) as it carries part of the burden of Jesus' thought about God as Redeemer. We introduce this with a few comments upon his ideas about the destiny of the individual at the time of his death. This is to a great extent involved in the larger question, but it is also relevant to the subject of sin and forgiveness.

With regard to the question of life after death, Jesus was a thoroughgoing Pharisee. He took for granted the idea of resurrection the Pharisees held. He was most explicit about this in the discussion into which he was forced by certain Sadducees. They tried to confuse Jesus by imagining an absurd possibility. Seven brothers in succession had the same woman as wife in this life, they said. Continuing, they asked: "In the resurrection whose wife will she be?" Driving through the underbrush to the essential issues, Jesus replied: "Is not this why you are wrong, that you know neither the scriptures nor the power of God?" By assuming in a quotation that the patriarchs were still alive, Jesus repudiated the interpretation of the scriptures the Sadducees championed. Then he implied that God's wisdom and power were equal to the contingency indicated by them, and that the problem could safely be left in his hands. What he actually said was that sex in human terms would not be a characteristic of the resurrected life, that different conditions would operate.

Jesus left the issue there. He did not speculate, as the Pharisees did, about details. Where he assumed certain details, as in the Parable of the Rich Man and Lazarus, he was simply reflecting popular conceptions. They were incidental to the spiritual and moral ideas he was emphasizing. He was quite content to leave to God matters about which only God could know the answers. This was his consistent attitude with regard to the speculative tendencies of Jewish thinkers, no matter what the issue. The discussion with the Sadducees is but one case in point. This becomes clear, as we shall presently observe, in his thought about the future hope in general.

The question of Jesus' thought about the future hope, or eschatology, is complex and baffling. There is abundant room for speculation and difference of opinion owing to the nature of the Gospel reports. We shall endeavor here to set down ideas of which we can be reasonably confident. Even then, however, we shall undoubtedly oversimplify the matter and, because there is no choice, be offering a very speculative conclusion. At least what we suggest will be consistent with Jesus' scale of values that we have up to this point elucidated. At times oversimplification serves a useful purpose, if it meets the condition of a reasonable coherence with related factors.

In advancing upon this topic we assume that the so-called "Little Apocalypse" of Mark 13 (and parallels in Matthew and Luke) is not the best place to begin. The influence of early Christian interpretation is very evident here, and the chapter is not consistent with itself. Its value must be tested with reference to other, more authentic materials in the Gospels.

In the light of Jesus' background there is only one debatable question. There can be no reasonable doubt but that he shared the general view of the future consummation of God's purposes with which the expectation of Judaism was saturated. Unless we are going to throw out some of Jesus' most characteristic sayings, which appear abundantly in every source, we must take that for granted. The only doubt attaches to the type of future expectation that enlisted his sympathies. Specifically, was he a nationalist, an apocalyptist, a prophet, a combination of any two or three of these, or none of them? This is the only real issue.

There are those who question whether Jesus had an eschatology at all in the sense in which we have assumed him to be genuinely a son of Judaism. The problem concerns his alleged predictions of a final judgment that would bring history to an end. Various "vehicle" theories offer an interpretation that cannot be fitted into Jesus' setting. John's Gospel was one of the earliest of these. Judgment comes in personal religious experience when men stand in the presence of Christ, the Light shining in the darkness. For Augustine the coming of God's reign was equated with the institution of the Church. Christ would not come in the future. He had already come in his Church. Modern scholars have echoed these assumptions in various ways. There may be value in such theories as signifying the meaning for religious experience that Jesus came to have, but they do not help us in our efforts to interpret the mind of the earthly Jesus. In his eschatology as in everything else he was a native son of Israel. We simply confuse the issue by assuming anything else.

The real issue, we have said, is what type of future hope characterized Jesus' thought. One thing only is clear at the beginning. That is that Jesus fits no category of thought in his environment exactly. He is in touch with them all, influenced by them all, yet not wholly of any one. He comes closest to the classical prophetic outlook, but not in all respects. Here as everywhere else he is strictly himself. This will become evident as we take each potential category in turn and conclude with his distinctive emphases.

Consider first the idea of nationalistic hope. Nothing is more certain than that Jesus had nothing to do with a view of the future that emphasized, or even included, nationalistic exclusiveness. He had no sympathy with the underground and its agitation for armed revolt against Rome. The Triumphal Entry is very instructive with regard to this. Dorothy Sayers' dramatization of the event is also good interpretation. In her play Captain Baruch of the Zealots, upon learning that Jesus is coming to the Passover, dictates the following letter to him:

Baruch the Zealot, to Jesus of Nazareth, the Son of David, King of Israel, greeting. I have observed you, and I know who you are. To every man opportunity comes once and not again. The Priests and Pharisees are in league to deliver you to Rome; but the people are on your side, and I have men and arms. Give me a sign, for now is the moment to strike and seize your kingdom. When a king comes in peace, he rides upon an ass; but when he goes to war, upon a horse. In the stable of Zimri, at the going-up into the City, is a war-horse saddled and ready. Set yourself upon him, and you shall ride into Jerusalem with a thousand spears behind you. But if you refuse, then take the ass's colt that is tied at the vineyard door, and Baruch will bide his time till a bolder Messiah come.

Jesus' answer is obvious. He chose the ass. Matthew interpreted this by means of a passage from Zechariah (9:9) that may well have been in Jesus' mind. John's Gospel brings out the essential thought of Jesus when it quotes his words: "My kingship is not of this world; if my kingship were of this world, my servants would fight."

The chief stumbling block to any theory of nationalistic messiah-ship on Jesus' part is his choice of the path of suffering rather than that of the sword. His future hope had nothing in common with that which dreamed of national glory won by force of arms. An ambiguous saying of Jesus mentions Davidic messiahship, but we cannot tell exactly what it means. Against the background of his choice of the cross it is evident that, except perhaps in a purely formal way, Jesus did not view himself as Son of David.

His sayings about the future judgment make his outlook explicit. That judgment would be a moral trial, nothing more and nothing less. The only criterion of judgment would be evidence of obedience to God's will in terms of the love that Jesus made central to the definition of obedience. Many sayings already cited have indicated this. Direct references to the future judgment simply nail down the hatch. They are abundant. The Parable of the Rich Man and Lazarus is typical. How one has treated human need is all that matters. The Parable of the Great Judgment is even more forceful on that point. Humanitarian sympathies and activities of a very practical nature are the sole criteria of the separation of sheep and goats. Nothing is even implied about distinctions of nationality, race, sex, social status, and other accidents of existence. In Jesus' denunciations cities of Judaism, including Jerusalem, share the same fate as non-Judaic cities. Privileged classes within the nation stand on the same ground as the

less favored. Harlots who repent precede proud Pharisees into the
kingdom. Without exception the criteria of judgment are spiritual and
moral in nature. Favored-nation status or nationalistic privilege is
completely irrelevant. By implication any type of special privilege,
except spiritual and moral worth, is as irrelevant as Countee Cullen's
"For a Lady I Know" suggests:

> She even thinks that up in heaven
> Her class lies late and snores,
> While poor black cherubs rise at seven
> To do celestial chores.

Any Jew who thought that the Gentiles would at the End be dele-
gated to the status of doing "celestial chores" for the Chosen People
was, according to Jesus, to be sadly disillusioned.

The crucial issue in this area of thought concerns Jesus' reactions
to the apocalypticism that flourished in his environment. We have
previously reviewed the ways in which this type of future hope deviated from that of the classical prophets, at the same time that it
grew out of it and shared its basic tenets. The test to be applied to
Jesus is here suggested. If he was a thoroughgoing apocalyptist, the
Gospels should make these deviations from the prophetic outlook
stand out in his teaching. However, the Gospels do not do so. The
most distinctive features of the apocalyptic hope are minor and ambiguous notes in the total picture of Jesus in the Gospels. Furthermore, they exist on the whole in parts of the Gospels that are most
obviously highly interpreted by the early Christians. Mark 13 is the
chief example, but it does not stand alone. The most that can be
said is that Jesus was influenced by the ideas and the phraseology of
this way of viewing the future hope, but his characteristic emphases
were elsewhere.

In order to make this clear, we shall review briefly the thought of
Jesus with reference to the major deviations of apocalyptic thought
from that of the prophets. The former transferred the scene of the
struggle between God and Satan to the transcendent sphere, and gave
it cosmic dimensions it did not have in prophetic thought. There
are reflections of such ideas in Jesus' words. They include mentions
of angels, demons, and Satan. Mark especially makes a point of in-

terpreting Jesus' exorcism of demons in cosmic proportions. Over against Satan and his legions of demons stand God and his Spirit. Jesus is endowed with the Spirit at Baptism. By the power of the Spirit he subdues Satan in the Temptation. When accused by his opponents of working in the power of Beelzebub (Satan), he refutes the charge. He does not deny the existence of demons, but he says that one who works for Satan would not be fighting the demons as he obviously is. A house internally divided cannot stand. He even claims that in casting out demons he is demonstrating the power of God's Spirit at work in him. Jesus may well have viewed this aspect of his work within the context of a cosmic struggle. If so, each successful exorcism of a demon would have been for him victory in one battle in the cosmic conflict. It would also have been for him evidence that the New Age was being introduced. However, this is not exclusively apocalyptic in meaning. Jesus' evident compassion for the needy must also have operated in this type of healing. Furthermore, we can never be sure of the extent to which this aspect of his work has been inaccurately interpreted by Mark. When we have the demons recognizing Jesus' divine status, a fact hidden from others, we are evidently in the presence of interpretation after the event.

A series of Son of man passages coheres with this general aspect of apocalyptic thought. The most emphatic is: "And then they will see the Son of man coming in clouds with great power and glory" to gather "his elect." The problem of the Son of man sayings has been dealt with in Chapter II. It was indicated that it is insoluble as to whether Jesus ever said anything about a Son of man, and, if he did, whether he had himself in mind. At least we must look elsewhere for more convincing evidence of his thought.

One thing at least is clear. Jesus did not share the idea basic to apocalypticism that God was exclusively transcendent. For him God had not ceased all activity in the present. He was not just waiting to act in a cataclysmic ending of history. He was near and approachable. We need not repeat what has been said on this point. It represents a serious challenge to the view that Jesus was exclusively an apocalyptist.

Another facet of the apocalyptic view was the belief that the End would be preceded by a program of melancholy events, the Messianic Woes. Mark 13 fits into this view, although inconsistently, as well as a few other stray sayings of Jesus. Among the latter are exhortations to be wise in interpreting the weather and the signs of the times and such a saying as that about bringing fire and divisions on the earth. No one of these sayings, however, has an exclusive apocalyptic bearing. Even the Mark 13 references may originally, to the extent that they come from Jesus at all, have had a nonapocalyptic intent. For example, Mark has Jesus refer to "the desolating sacrilege." This is Daniel's symbol for the altar to the Olympian Zeus erected in the temple by Antiochus IV. The Lucan parallel to this Marcan saying takes this to mean Jerusalem under siege, a historical event. Luke may be reading back after the fall of Jerusalem in A.D. 70, but his interpretation of Mark shows that the "desolating sacrilege" was not exclusively apocalyptic in connotation.

Among more authentic notes is Jesus' blunt assertion that "no sign shall be given," unless it is "the sign of Jonah." The latter was the preaching of repentance, the call to decision in the present, not a forecast of something to come. The sign of the reign of God for Jesus was his own message and work. This connection was eschatological. That is, it had to do with the fulfillment of God's purpose. But it was not apocalyptic in form. The presence of the reign of God by anticipation in Jesus' words and deeds, including demon exorcism, is the force of the saying: "The kingdom of God is not coming with signs to be observed; nor will they say, 'Lo, here it is!' or 'There!' for behold, the kingdom of God is in the midst of you." The "atmospheric pressure" of the coming reign, its radar finding, is Jesus himself. There is a predictive element here, but it is no more apocalyptic than Amos' prediction of doom upon Israel many years earlier.

Apocalypticism also worked upon the idea of a fixed schedule of events with regard to the future consummation. It was as rigid as the flight schedule of a modern air line. Deviations were at times permitted, but only as the tower directed. God might shorten the days, or lengthen them, for the sake of the Elect, but the basic structure remained rigid. Some sayings of Jesus conform in a general way to this pattern. Equivocal Son of man sayings are among them, such as, "You will not have gone through all the towns of Israel, before the Son of man comes." The Passion predictions are in that mold. The equation of John the Baptist with Elijah, the messiah's forerunner, cohere. Certain "crisis parables" imply this perspective. Their theme is: "Watch therefore—for you do not know when the master of the house will come." Unexpectedness rather than certainty appears to be the thought, but the implication is that the return of the master will be very soon. This is roughly to believe that he is coming on a prearranged schedule. The servants may be in the dark about it, but not the master himself. Not to know "the day or the hour" means to be uncertain only about the split second.

Some of this material can be dismissed as interpretation by early Christians, but not all. The Mark 13 sayings and the Passion predictions indicate an element of hindsight, but the thought of an un-expected and sudden event about to take place is thoroughly embedded in the tradition. What gives significance to this is that an apocalyptic End, such as might be implied here, did not take place. It did not come at all. This posed a serious problem for early Christians who thought that Jesus had predicted such an End. In the face of that, it is unlikely that they would have invented sayings that proved Jesus to have been mistaken. On the other hand, among some at least, the expectation was strong that Jesus would return soon, and that he himself had predicted his coming. I Thessalonians takes this for granted, and Matthew's Gospel shows the influence of this view. General sayings of Jesus with reference to the future in Mark are changed by Matthew to an explicit statement about Jesus' "coming." Other strains of early Christian thought toned this aspect of the matter down. We see this most notably in John's Gospel and the Acts of the Apostles. Thus early Christians were not agreed about the subject of Jesus' return, and the records of what he said are themselves not unambiguous about it. At least we are aware of a great sense of urgency in his message. There is the expectation of some great act of God about to be performed. It was probably the prophetic tendency to foreshorten the time until judgment, grounded in moral sensitivity. It may have been more in the mood of transcendental eschatology. We do not know, and the question must remain open.

We cannot settle the question without recourse to other words of Jesus. However, one thing is unambiguous, and it tells us much more than we can learn from equivocal sayings that leave us uncertain. There is nothing in the Gospels of the speculation, going to fantastic lengths, that characterized apocalyptic prediction. There is no claim to know God's schedule of events about the future any more than there is interest in wondering about the details of the destiny of the individual. These matters Jesus leaves to God. "No sign shall be given" is what he says, and this accords with his humility and sense of realism in all matters. Concentrated as he was upon the decision that God in the present was demanding of men, it is unlikely that he would have thought it important to know God's schedule, or even whether he had one of an inflexible nature.

The case against the theory that Jesus was an apocalyptic fanatic is clinched when we review the form of thought and expression that characterized this way of thinking. Visions, esoteric prophecies, and the like are its stock in trade. These are minor notes in the Gospels. The symbolism of apocalypticism that we noted previously is not Jesus' customary way of expressing himself. The difference between almost any apocalypse and Jesus' sayings in the Sermon on the Mount and in his parables is as great as that between the arctic regions and the tropics. If he was not an apocalyptist in this respect, how could he have been an apocalyptist in others? Except for minor influences Jesus does not fit the pattern at all. A survey of his parables confirms this. He did use symbols. The parable itself was a symbol. It was an imaginative story designed to impart an idea about God's nature and functioning or about human conduct. But—it was a vignette of real life. Men were actually robbed on the barren Jericho Road. Farmers did sow and reap, and sheep did get lost. The use of the parable form implies a theory of divine revelation different from that of the apocalyptists. They imply that God's mind could be read in the most commonplace things of daily life, if one was spiritually alert and morally sensitive.

Jesus is set apart from apocalyptic views, just as from nationalistic aspirations, by his act of suffering. As we have said, the "heavenly man" idea was that the messiah would come in triumph, not suffering as a means to that end. If Jesus used the term Son of man at all, it is most likely that the precedent of Psalm 8 or of Ezekiel was in his mind, combined perhaps with Suffering Servant. In Psalm 8 "son of man" is equivalent to "man." The transition from "man" as the object of attention on the Sabbath to "the Son of man" as "Lord of the Sabbath" can be seen in Mark 2:27–28. Matthew and Luke omit the former and retain the latter. If Jesus viewed himself as in some way the sign of the dawning reign of God, he might have been in-

skillfully and radically. The fundamental elements of human nature are the same in every age, and the basic questions men ask about their existence do not change from culture to culture. On this deeper level Jesus lived and worked and thought. His teaching was not philosophical, not pedantic, not technical. It was popular, picturesque, practical. His thinking was religious rather than theological. He appealed to experience rather than to speculation. He forced spiritual and moral, rather than intellectual, decisions on men. He stressed principles rather than practical programs. His claim to authority was of the same nature. He did not rely upon the sword, forcing a reluctant allegiance. He did not appeal to theory, compelling the intellect to yield a point in a debate. Titles by means of which to define his status were comparatively unimportant to him. What mattered was his religious and moral challenge. He appealed to the experience of men, to their deepest intuitions and insights. He asked men to test him, to find out for themselves whether or not he spoke truly. Men have done just that. They have tested him in every time and place and found him true, true in terms of the quality of his insight and of his life. So he speaks to us today, asking us to test him. But he does more than that. Because of his immeasurable greatness he forces us to decision for or against him—that is, for or against the God he reveals. We may turn away, but we cannot avoid him. This is the wonder of Jesus.

It is this fact that provides the necessity and the orientation of the present chapter. Since we must make a decision about him in the realm of faith, it is important to know what it is that we are asked to decide. This whole book, as we have said, proceeds upon the basis of that presupposition. It seeks to provide the data upon the basis of which the decision of faith may be an enlightened one. Everything that has been written up to this point, to the extent that it represents a valid portrait of Jesus, contributes to that end. It stands in its own right. It is self-authenticating and challenging without being moralized, just as the memory of Lincoln makes its direct impact upon us. The only reason for carrying the exposition further is that there are so many different ideas today as to what it means to make the decision of faith with regard to Jesus.

"Christianity" is an omnibus term. It includes all manner of assorted ideas and practices, some of which are in flat contradiction to others. Its common denominator is a historical figure, a certain Jesus of Nazareth who came to be called Christ. Under that name, however, very diverse things take place. They are as far apart as the handling of poison snakes and relief programs for world refugees, the silence of Quaker worship and the elaborate rites of Eastern Orthodoxy. The term "Christian" is in that respect like the term "Democrat" in American politics. A political Democrat may be a southern reactionary or a Socialist. The only thing they have in common is a label and a common desire to elect a candidate for public office who bears that label. "Democracy" itself is such a label. It may signify what a Communist means by it or what a proponent of the "American Dream" means by it, and they are hardly identical except in terminology. Before it means anything its content must be defined. In the same way "Christianity" today is a label. It means different things to different people.

Because of that it may serve a useful purpose to draw out some of the implications of our historical study with reference to today's world—at least as one individual sees them. In doing so we have Christians primarily in mind. On the other hand, in so doing one is, indirectly at least, addressing anyone who cares to listen. This is inevitable in the nature of the case, because the subject of study is a figure with universal dimensions.

The need for such an exposition is obvious enough. Yet one hesitates, at least momentarily, to essay the task assigned both by logic and conscience. There is a certain flavor of presumptuousness about it. As has been indicated, there is a highly personal aspect to what one must say. He can make only his own affirmation of faith. Of greater moment is the fact that no one individual can know enough about his world to speak with authority on many pertinent issues. His opinions are those of one person and subject to many limitations.

There is also the fact that, in a very true sense, it is impossible for anyone to tell another just what Jesus can or will mean to him. That is a matter of personal experience involving the secret depths of the individual's mind and heart. This is in part what Albert Schweitzer expressed so well when he wrote: "He comes to us as One unknown, without a name, as of old, by the lake-side, He came to those who knew Him not. He speaks to us the same word: 'Follow thou me!' and sets us to the tasks which He has to fulfill for our time." No single individual can know ahead of time exactly what part he will be asked to play in "the tasks which He has to fulfill for our time," let alone tell another what his role should be. There is an inevitable personal equation. The conditioning of inheritance, environment, and previous experience contributes an individual aspect to our perception that cannot be avoided. Opportunity limits and defines the area and the extent of our performance. The man without college training can hardly serve his age as college teacher or doctor. One who is blind cannot fly an airplane. Age as well as ability narrows the area in which one can work effectively. Factors of many kinds predetermine our task in many respects. What Jesus can and will mean to the individual is bound up with all this. No generalization can cover every facet of this highly personal and individual aspect of Jesus' coming.

There is still another consideration. Only the individual can make his own decision of faith as he confronts the challenge of Jesus. A decision must be made, since Jesus' stature leaves us with "no place to hide." The decision is one to action. "What will you *do* with me?" is the form it takes. It involves what we think about him and how we feel about him, but it is fundamentally a challenge to action, to a life. "Follow me!" is the way Jesus put it. He also said, "Why do you call me 'Lord, Lord' and not *do* what I tell you?" It is more a matter of courage than of thought. It is the actual leap into the water off the end of the diving board, into water over our head. It is testing for ourselves what we have seen others do and what our reason tells us is possible for us too. This is a highly personal matter. It involves and affects one's fellow men, and it is made in the presence of a "cloud of witnesses." But essentially it is made in the presence of God on our own. No one else can make it for us.

For these reasons one hesitates to delve further into what Jesus may mean to another. It is, however, a momentary hesitation. One recalls the value to him of the testimony of many individuals, in humble as well as prominent station, to something they have seen and heard. He feels the compulsion of everyone who has been constrained to bear witness to the most important thing in his life. Furthermore, all that can be done is to offer what has been seen and heard to the testing of the reason and the experience of others. No one can be compelled to listen, let alone to agree.

Two basic convictions give body to this sense of constraint. They have both been reiterated already in the course of our presentation. Thus they need no more than passing mention. The one is that Jesus is the religious ultimate, the hope of our distressed world. The other represents the narrower thesis of this book. With reference to Schweitzer's statement, it is the idea that Jesus cannot come to us entirely "unknown" or he does not come at all. If he does not come with distinctive marks of individuality, words have lost their meaning. He cannot set us to tasks to fulfill for him in our day that are inconsistent with ideas, ideals, and values that were his food and drink. His tasks today must, from the standpoint of values, be those he set himself to fulfill in his own time. None of this makes any sense, however, unless we have a concrete image before our minds.

We do have such an image. Previous chapters have sought to make its characteristic features stand out. It might help us to summarize that image at this point, but that would be needless repetition. Having it in mind as it has been presented, we proceed to the constructive part of our task.

The first thing we learn from Jesus relative to our day is in the nature of a general observation. It is the extremely important observation that Jesus comes to us not with specific solutions of practical problems, but with vertical vision. It applies directly and practically to the horizontal plane of real life, but it does not relieve us of thought and planning in specific ways. It does not in any sense save us from deciding whether or not our child should be spanked or nuclear testing abandoned. Jesus offers us no quick answers as to how to solve the problems of juvenile delinquency or "the population explosion." He gives us no inside information as to whom we should try to elect to public office. He offers no magic formula for settling the conflict between the Communist and the Western dogmas, let alone any one of the units of the tangled skein of which it is the focal point. He gives no particular plan of a social, economic, or political nature the right to be called "Christian," at least not directly. Instead he comes as the religious ultimate, with a vision of God and the eternal values that he honors. He challenges us to believe that these values, for which he lived and died, represent the elemental stuff of the spiritual and moral universe. Thus his basic challenge is to believe something about God and, derived from that, something about man and his social relationships. He teaches absolutes in absolute terms. To that extent he offers ideals, not practical panaceas. At the same time these absolute values have to do with real life. After all, a man was not crucified in Jesus' society, any more than in ours, for dreaming nice things about God. Because he brought his scale of values into the market place he was a force to be dealt with. So it is today. He challenges us in practical ways, but in terms of foundations. He forces us to test every practical program by his scale of values, but he leaves to us just what that means.

At least one value of a study of Jesus in his ancient setting is thus made clear. This saves us from asking the wrong questions and from expecting answers he cannot give. It saves us from a barren literalism that takes his words out of historical context and plants them in modern soil that cannot sustain them. As though whether Jesus baptized has anything to do with the question of its feasibility today! If he did, as though the form he employed has the slightest relevance to how we should perform the act! As though whether Jesus was a "pacifist" in his social milieu has any bearing upon the issue in its modern form! Jesus himself reinforces common sense to teach us a better way to learn what he is trying to say to us today.

We cannot stop, however, with this general observation. It is fundamental, but it is not all that can be said. With reference to current thinking and practice, we can learn something of a very specific nature from the Historical Jesus that we cannot learn elsewhere. He guides us unerringly in our efforts to fill the term "Christian" with a distinctive content. He teaches us to distinguish between authentic and unauthentic reflections of his mind and spirit in the welter of voices being dinned into our ears today. He is the only one who can accomplish this crucial effect.

The attempt to be more specific runs the risk of unwarranted modernization of Jesus, but we have no choice. The question is not whether we should modernize, but only how we shall do it. Just as in the formation of presuppositions, there is a right way and a wrong way. There is the way that is based upon evidence and that which is based upon wishful thinking. That is the test. The whole impact of this book is in the direction of informed presuppositions, and thus of intelligent modernization.

Three comprehensive areas of modern thought and practice will be considered in working out this theme. They involve problems of crucial importance. In each case we ask what it means when the light of Jesus' vertical vision is permitted to shine upon the issues. Or, we seek authentic notes of his penetrating thought and spirit. The areas selected are simply examples of what Jesus may mean in any area of thought and practice. We seek only to indicate a point of view, not to exhaust an involved subject.

## THE CHRISTIAN CHURCH

The place to begin, it would seem, is with the organized Church that exists in Jesus' name. The question to be asked is, "What are the genuine marks of discipleship as judged by Jesus himself?" His answer is quite unambiguous. It is in the form of what should be emphasized, not what should be included or excluded in the paraphernalia of organized religion. That is, he challenges us to place the emphasis where he placed it, upon the spiritual and moral values he embodied. This he sets over against theological and ecclesiastical forms and labels. Jesus gives no institution or individual the right to call itself by his name unless that is its standard and its practice. The same holds for a nation or a civilization. He does not thereby tell us what we should do about the necessities of organization in a world such as ours. He has no direct word about clerical orders, sacraments, or administrative machinery. These are all required for the effective expression of religion. They are inevitable in the nature of life. Jesus concerns himself with only one thing: the heart of the organization. The nature of true discipleship is what matters to him, because nothing else matters if the root of the tree is not sound. Nothing is gained when smooth-running machinery is employed to an end inconsistent with his spirit. The heart of a true Christian church is the individual, joined with others, who, out of an experience of God's grace in his heart, gives himself without reservation to God's service of love among men. That is the sole and exclusive test of whether an institution is or is not a Church of Christ.

What does this mean with reference to our creeds, especially their formulations of Jesus' significance? Jesus does not discourage speculation about his person. It is inevitable, life being what it is. All that he says is that it is all meaningless unless it meets one condition. That condition is that, in motivation and in form, it be a genuinely appreciative and intelligent response to his spiritual and moral genius. The particular forms this response may take are passing. Only the spiritual and moral foundation abides. How to explain his greatness is secondary to conforming one's life to its demands. This means that if two men talk the same language on the spiritual and moral level, they are true disciples, however much they may differ in intellectual ways of defining or praising his stature. The former is crucial. The latter may be irrelevant.

This has far-reaching and radical implications for the Christian churches in their interrelationships and in their confrontation of other world religions. The same principle applies to both areas. Mutuality with regard to love of God and man, as exemplified by Jesus, is the only test of fellowship with him. Like every leader worthy of a following, he wanted his cause supported, and his cause was God's work in human history. How men thought of his status was important only as it contributed to that end. Jesus never even implied that before God, in judgment now or later, any question is raised about one's formal religious affiliations. The labels are not considered because they are irrelevant. They are inclusive terms meaning different things to different people. This was as true of "Jew" and "Gentile" in Jesus' day as of "Christian" and "non-Christian" today. The essence is all that matters to God. No individual will have any advantage in judgment because of a label, be it "Protestant," "Roman Catholic," "Orthodox," or "Christian," "Hindu," "Muslim." These are usually the accidents of environment. Each individual and institution is judged in the light of its opportunities and talents on the basis of one criterion alone: have one's fellow men been loved as God loves them? Have they been loved from the heart and with intelligent activity? That at least is where Jesus placed his emphasis, and he did it with great intensity. Why should we think that his challenge is different today?

Certainly Paul interpreted Jesus in this way. The setting was Jew (circumcision) versus Gentile (uncircumcision), but the principle was the same then as now. The way Paul said it was in these terms: "For neither is circumcision anything, nor uncircumcision, but a new creation." A great modern thinker, Paul Tillich, has expressed what this means with reference to our theme (*The New Being*, pp. 16 ff.):

Christianity in the present world encounters several forms of circumcision and uncircumcision. Circumcision can stand today for everything called religion, uncircumcision for everything called secular, but making half-religious claims. . . . [Paul] says: No particular religion matters, neither ours nor yours. But I want to tell you that something has happened that matters, something that judges . . . your religion and my religion. A New Creation has occurred. . . . And so we should say to pagans and Jews wherever we meet them: Don't compare your religion and our religion. . . . All this is of no avail. And above all don't think that we want to convert you to English or American Christianity, to the religion of the Western World. We do not want to convert you to us, not even to the best of us. This would be of no avail. We want only to show you something we have seen and to tell you something we have heard: That in the midst of the old creation there is a New Creation, and that this New Creation is manifest in Jesus who is called the Christ.

This is the authentic voice of what is called the Kerygma, the proclamation of the saving power of God through Jesus. It is authentic because it tells us that Jesus is more than an ancient Jewish prophet of unique proportions. He is one who, in some way or other, comes to us in our day with enlightenment and power. That is one side of the matter. It is authentic also because it does not neglect the other side of the shield. It proclaims the fact that "this New Creation is manifest in Jesus who is called the Christ." He is "called the Christ," but it is Jesus who is so named, Jesus of Nazareth. We know the nature of the New Creation in and through his living spirit because we first know him in history.

The preaching of the Kerygma loses its force when that is forgotten. It is forgotten or neglected when we are told that we confront Jesus only, or almost so, in proclamations of faith. The danger here is that we may substitute exaggerated claims for him in theological terms for his true challenge. It is possible to profess faith in Jesus with a fanatical dogmatism and still deny his real spirit. We can exalt a figment of our own imagination that says much more about our prejudices than about Jesus. We not only can, we do. In greater or less degree this is what has been done by professed followers of Jesus in every generation. It is still being done by all of us. The difference is that some are more aware of it than others because they keep Jesus steadily in view, and are able as a result to keep correcting their perspective.

It is not hard to understand why Christians deny Jesus in this manner. They deny him for the same reason that Peter did. Confronted by the austere demands of the real Jesus, Peter was confused and afraid. He was afraid to let go of his prejudices, the old creation, and submit himself to Jesus' rigorous discipline. The challenge of Jesus was a radical one, and it still is. It is nothing more or less than the challenge to complete self-abandonment, complete outgoing love, and that has always been a very rugged demand in our kind of world. It is no wonder that we refuse to face Jesus in all his glory, his divinity, because it is at the same time an extremely rugged manhood. It is much easier to call him "Lord, Lord," and think that we can thereby escape his real challenge. We escape into theology or religious experience or "peace of mind."

This is all very negative, but, when the occasion called for it, Jesus was quite negative too. His message of judgment held out not the slightest hope for this type of superficiality, and his criticism of the religious leaders of Judaism was stern indeed. The only reason for emphasizing this feature of Jesus' message is that today we tend to hide from it as we seek security under the pressure of events. We do not often betray Jesus overtly, as Judas did. We just ignore him. We don't pound nails through his hands and feet. We just let him go alone to Calvary. We turn our backs. That is, our indifference takes the form of lip service. We name his name, but ignore him in terms of the values for which he lived and died. We use his name to justify our smallness, our cowardice, our selfishness. He is nothing but a label. Blasphemy is the proper word for all this. It is the only form of heresy that Jesus condemned. Struggles for power within the churches called heresy trials mean little to him. He was the victim of one! He digs deeper, as always. Weakness he could forgive, but not the use of his name to justify thought and conduct that violated everything he considered important enough to die for. With pathos, but with finality, he passes his judgment still: "How often would I have gathered thy children together, . . . but you would not! Behold, your house is forsaken!"

The other side of this shield is more encouraging. There are many today who do understand his challenge and who seek to respond to it with sincerity and courage. They are usually humble in demeanor, realizing more acutely than others how far short they fall of his standard. But they have committed themselves to his service in great or in small ways, depending upon their talents and opportunities. Like Schweitzer, they lose their lives in service to their fellows, finding their lives as a result. The forms of this service are as varied as life itself. They range from the kitchen sink to high political office. However different they may be, they are expressions of what Paul called the one Body of Christ, infused and inspired with the same Spirit. These disciples are ready to pay the price of the discipline to which Jesus calls them, since the price is great in a world like ours—as great as it was in first century Palestine. The path of genuine love has never been easy. Jesus did not indicate that it was. The cross signifies that. Knowing all that, his true disciples have discovered something more important. They have learned, in the words of the earlier quotation, that a New Creation has come to pass through Jesus. They have discovered that along this path lies the peace of God. This is not the aspirin-tablet type of "peace of mind" so falsely advocated today by some as the sum and substance of the Christian Gospel. The peace of God does not save us from a cross any more than it saved Jesus. It does not exist, paradoxically enough, except in the heart that is disturbed and broken by man's inhumanity to man. It is the blessing upon the heart that suffers such pain, when the life involved is being spent to do something about the hurt that others experience. Thus it is the pearl of great price, its glory subduing every hardship and every other lesser value.

This noble company is by no means identical with formal Christianity. "Christianity" is not a criterion of value or of reality. It is just a label, defining nothing. As we have previously indicated, the great judgment scene gives no attention whatsoever to labels. One is not even asked about his attitude toward Jesus. The point here is that those who received the King's blessing were surprised. When had they contributed anything to the King? When had they fed and clothed him or attended him in sickness or imprisonment? They couldn't remember. They had been doing this so constantly that one recipient of their good will did not stand out above another. And some of those to whom they had given themselves could hardly have been Jesus! Some were prostitutes. Others were filthy and ragged and foul-mouthed. Some were young people with bitterness toward society, so bitter that they killed and raped. The King's response dissolved the quandary: "As you did it to one of the least of these my brethren, you did it to me." The open heart, the compassionate heart, turning away from all selfish advantage and finding constructive ways to implement its feelings—this is the sole criterion of judgment. These persons are found both within and without the institution that goes under Jesus' banner. In fact they constitute his Church, used in the singular. In them is to be found the hope of the world, because only in this form can Jesus fulfill the tasks for our day assigned to him by the God he served and whose essential character he manifested.

In expressing such sentiments one is not carrying on a crusade against organized religion. In our world it cannot take any other form any more than it could in Jesus' day. Jesus himself organized his group, with twelve men selected out of many for special purposes. One would even have to admit that an organization by its very nature involves waste and compromise. This is human life, not heaven! Nor would one wish to be guilty of failing to appreciate the tremendous contributions of the churches to the meeting of human need. From one point of view this is phenomenal, whether in the expenditure of money or of human lives. There is a type of criticism of the churches that needs to be repudiated. Whatever the darker side of the picture, the spirit of Jesus has been present in the midst of his organized disciples over the centuries. It is an honorable record. It is only with the darker side that we are concerned. There are those who have not learned to put first things first with reference to Jesus' scale of values. Some of them are very active in church affairs, but they do not know that activity as such is simply the expenditure of energy. It may or may not serve Jesus' purposes. It may be a means of escaping serious consideration of Jesus' demands upon them.

In the face of the world revolution that is going on, signifying the birth of a new day for mankind, one wants the Church to which he belongs and which he loves to rise to its great hour. Embodying the real spirit of Jesus, it can lead mankind wisely to its true destiny. Denying its Master, it can guarantee chaos and frustration, even its annihilation. That is the challenge of Jesus. It is also the reason for taking it so seriously.

## SCIENCE AND RELIGION

The Greeks, not the Hebrews, were the early scientists. Like his ancestors and his contemporaries, Jesus showed no scientific interest in nature or human life in the modern sense of the term. He was no Aristotle. Granting that, he has something to contribute in this area of thought.

The first thing we may consider is what he has to say to those who, often in his name, attack the whole enterprise of modern science. They are disturbed by what appears to be conflict between the science of the Bible and modern concepts. The theory of evolution especially disturbs them. It seems to deny the science of Genesis. Jesus comes into this picture to the extent that he apparently took the views of Genesis for granted. To accept the views of modern science is to deny him, it is said.

To take this position is to misread the spirit of Jesus. The views of Jesus about science are irrelevant to the question of what we should believe today. He took for granted the science of Genesis just like every other first century Jew. How could he have done anything else? He never claimed to be an authority in this area. He claimed only that God was of a certain nature, spiritually and morally speaking. The implication was that he remained that way no matter what men thought about the mechanics of his creative activity. It is impossible to believe that any discovery of modern science would phase him, whether it be that of Darwin or of Freud. More than that, it is impossible not to believe that he would welcome any light upon the mechanics of God's creative activity. In the spiritual realm, which was his interest, he expanded his thought of God in line with prophetic views far beyond that of his contemporaries. Would he not do the same thing in the realm of science, if there was sufficient reason to do so? How much greater is the glory of the Creator from the perspective of modern science than from that of ancient science! His majesty is breath-taking. Jesus surely would welcome this, without taking his eyes off the spiritual and moral factors that are primary.

The attack on modern science that is being treated here does not really rest upon appreciation of Jesus. It arises upon a presupposition about the nature of the Bible that the spirit of Jesus rejects. It is assumed that God has said his last word about science as well as about religion in the Bible. It takes a literalistic view of scripture that Jesus repudiated. He did not repudiate it in the realm of science, but of spiritual and ethical matters. He held in theory a view of the Bible that may be called literalistic, but in practice he denied it. He denied it in favor of direct revelation in experience. If he denied it in the religious realm, he would also deny it in any other realm provided that there was sufficient reason for so doing. There was no reason for him to challenge the science of the Bible. The question was not alive as yet. Even if it had been, he might not have dealt with it, simply because his interests were elsewhere. But his spirit would not have hindered those who did. He was too creative a spirit to have been bound by any static theory about a Book or about anything else. Thus Jesus challenges the literalist to discover his mind in the spirit rather than in the letter.

On the other hand, Jesus has something to say to those who claim too much for science. We do not need Jesus, of course, to tell us that science, properly defined, is an intellectual instrument in man's control that he can use either for good or for evil. It is a method of finding things out about the natural universe and man's physical and mental make-up, on the basis of which reasonable predictions can be made. It can be extremely useful, curing our diseases and lightening our burdens. On the other hand, it can contribute technological unemployment or wipe out all life on the globe. Science as science cannot predetermine whether its effects will be beneficial or destructive. It is not a philosophy or a religion. When it forsakes its proper role it becomes "scientism," making many assumptions about the nature of life that it cannot demonstrate by scientific method. As we have said, we do not need Jesus to give us this information. In certain senses we do not need him to tell us some of the things still to be said, but there is value in considering his outlook. At least we can see what his challenge is.

Jesus reminds us that the questions with which science concerns itself are not of primary importance. Questions that have to do with the meaning of our existence are the basic ones. These questions abide through all changes in the level of our scientific understanding of life. They will abide when interplanetary travel is a reality, if it already isn't in some far corner of the universe. They will be those of greatest urgency when, if ever, psychology has complete understanding of what makes a person tick. As long as human nature is what it has always been, this will be true. The challenge of Jesus is to give primary attention to that which is primary. He demands that we give more time and energy to solving these basic dilemmas of human need than to acquiring know-how. Until we solve the former, all the know-how in the world is of no avail.

Within that context he reminds us that science is an instrument to be used for the benefit of man. It is to be judged not by the brilliance of its discoveries, but by its contributions to the health and the welfare of mankind. Nothing is gained by knowing how to do a bad thing better. There is gain only when good things are implemented. Surely then the spirit of Jesus stands behind every serious effort to work out the constructive uses of nuclear energy, just as it opposes every attempt to employ that awesome power selfishly. This does not mean that he gives us specific answers as to how it shall be done, whether, for example, we should or should not prepare more atomic warheads. He deals with values, not with precisely how they shall be implemented. The latter will take care of itself when head and heart are committed to true values. In the realm of healing, surely the spirit of Jesus urges the development of every means by which the bodies and the minds of men may be permitted fullness of life. This may take the form of an X-ray machine, medicines, or reliable psychiatric techniques. One does not follow Jesus by ignorance of the ways in which God works for healing today. Thus he supports, inspires rather, the pure science that lies behind the ability of men to create practical instruments for assistance to mankind.

His fundamental challenge comes at the point of motivation to this desirable end. It concerns our view of God and of man. He dares us to believe that God, despite the enlargement of our view of the universe, is the same Father he knew intimately in his own experience. He accepts the enlargement of our conception of God forced upon us by the new science. He glories in all this, since a God big enough to be able to handle any contingency in the universe we know is majestic indeed. But he still finds God's glory chiefly in the initiative he takes in behalf of human beings, their needs and their aspirations. To conclude that the God of our spacious universe is too transcendent to deal directly and intimately with his creatures is to repeat the mistake of those in Jesus' times whose views he qualified. Distance and size have nothing to do with values. This we know in human experience. This common sense joins with Jesus' outlook to strengthen our morale.

Near Srinagar in the Kashmir is a temple dedicated to a famous Hindu philosopher and teacher named Shankara. It stands high on a hill. Applied science has equipped it with fluorescent floodlights, so that at night it can be seen for miles around. It is a beacon, except that to receive the blessing it bestows the pilgrims must make a long climb. The deity it enshrines does not come down to them, even in the form of his priests. They must go to him. In Jesus' view, by contrast, God comes down. If we can no longer think of God as "up," it makes no difference. That he takes the initiative in seeking us out, as Jesus sought out publicans and sinners, still stands. That God came down, as it were, in the form of Jesus is basic to this. Floodlights or their absence, on temple or church, is an irrelevant consideration. It is a matter of spiritual reality, a reality unaffected by the progress of scientific thought. God's "body" may be differently conceived than in Jesus' day, but his "heart" is still the same. His transcendence is magnified, but he is not lost in the far reaches of the stellar universe. He seeks men still, meeting them on the ground of the same values as always. That at least is what Jesus challenges us to believe. Because it makes so much sense in terms of experience, it still moves us. It provides the morale we need in order to find the ways and means of adapting the gifts of science to our human existence in a beneficial manner.

Linked with this is Jesus' challenge to think optimistically about the nature of man. He directs us to the question of *what* man is in God's sight, refusing to be befuddled by the complexities of existence into stopping with the fact that man is. Man is made in the image of God, he said, and he asks us to remember it. This is not changed by the evidences of the demonic in man that recent history and modern psychology and psychiatry make clear enough. He knew all this when he gave himself on the cross believing that man was capable of responding to its impact. History has not proved him wrong. The recovery of Peter following Jesus' death is both a fact and a symbol. Men do have the capacity for heroism, even when their best efforts are clouded by inadequacy. Modern knowledge has deepened our understanding of the complex nature of man's psychology, but it has not eliminated his capacity to rise to selfhood consistent with Jesus' estimate of his being. Psychotherapeutic methods of treatment applied to juvenile delinquents, for example, show marked ability to help some to rise above their social conditioning. When medical and spiritual factors combine with this new technique, in any number of areas, the results are extremely encouraging. Jesus deals with none of this directly, but behind it all is his conviction that man is a spiritual being with infinite capacities bestowed by God himself. If he says anything more or less directly, it is that man can come to himself completely only when he acknowledges his spiritual birthright.

This bears upon the surge of mankind toward what we call democracy. In many areas of the world groups of people are not yet ready for democratic government in its Western form. Perhaps they never will be. They will discover their own form. Underneath and infused in this ferment is the presupposition that man has dignity before God. Without that premise there is no hope. Once again, the spirit of Jesus encourages men to believe that they were created for the dignity of self-government. He does not help us to decide in any given situation what the forms of democratic life should be. What he does do is to demand that efforts to work them out be made on the basis of an optimistic, if realistic, estimate of man's creative potentialities. In the face of every tyranny this is his challenge.

## THE SOCIAL EXPRESSION OF RELIGION

The term "Social Gospel" became prominent earlier in this century. It was, on the negative side, a protest against a conception of salvation that tended to overemphasize the private nature of religious experience. It affirmed, on the positive side, that the Christian Gospel had a message for the relationships of men in large groups. The Social Creeds of many churches today reflect this in the form of pronouncements relative to the whole gamut of social relationships. The items run from the family to international relationships. Some spokesmen for this point of view are even urging us to get prepared for interplanetary relationships.

This movement within modern Christianity has been disturbing to many. They attack the Social Creeds, especially the assumption that church as church has any business in these areas or that it can speak with a united voice. The Church may have the right to challenge its members to responsible citizenship, but not to be more specific. The Church includes both Republicans and Democrats, segregationists and integrationists, and opposite points of view on practically every public issue. Therefore, its role does not extend beyond the effort to inculcate within the individual the vision and the courage required for responsible participation in the affairs of the day. This is the best side of the attack. Others appear to believe that religion is more concerned with heaven than with this life. Still others are inconsistent. They agree that Christianity should have a social outreach, but within limits. It is right, for example, for the Church to be concerned with divorce or the liquor traffic, but not with the oil industry in Saudi Arabia or with problems of colored-white relations in South Africa. Still others appear to oppose this type of thought for no other reason than the wish to preserve things as they are or to return to some imagined Golden Age in the past.

Looked at from the angle of Jesus' literal example, there is much to be said for this position. Jesus did not have a social gospel in the modern sense of the term, any more than Paul did. The legalists whom he opposed were the proponents of a social gospel. That is, they sought a harmonious society by means of legislation. They sought to regulate every social relationship in this way in the name of religion. Jesus, by contrast, emphasized individual salvation. He was concerned with conduct, but his stress fell upon right motive and a disposition of good will. His controversies with the legalists mainly concerned strictly religious issues such as Sabbath observance. To the extent that he became involved in politics at all it was to take a rather passive attitude toward the Romans. His attack on the commercialism of the priests was religiously motivated, that temple worship might be pure. Thus the modern form of the Social Gospel cannot appeal to Jesus' literal example.

Having said this, we can immediately assert that it is entirely irrelevant to the modern issue. Our appeal to Jesus on this, as on every other, question is legitimate only as we seek to discover the implications of his basic ideas and attitudes. When we do that we face the fact that his religion is social to its core. It is a religion of love. Everything that has previously been said about this applies at this point. This means that no issue can be excluded from consideration when it is a question of the application of love. Furthermore, every issue must be included that involves the welfare of human beings. That is, love by its very nature demands a social gospel in the widest sense of that term. There is no other. Individuals equally devoted to love may differ over what it means in terms of its practical implementation with regard to any given issue, but they are followers of Jesus only to the extent that they agree on the basic premise.

The position of Jesus was similar to that of Paul. When the latter wrote his Letter to Philemon, dealing with the status of a slave before his master, he did not attack the system of slavery as such. He pleaded only for acceptance of the slave by the master in a spirit of love. There are any number of reasons why Paul did not carry on a crusade against the institution of slavery. Among the most important was the fact that a minority group like the Christians had no way of making their voice effective in government circles. However, the day came when they did, and the result was an end to slavery in the Roman Empire. Implicit in Paul's gospel of love was its application to such a social scourge as slavery. The same was true of Jesus' message from which Paul got his inspiration. The principle is that, when conditions make it feasible, love by its very nature requires practical implementation in every area of human relationships.

Not only is this evident from Jesus' exclusive emphasis upon love; it is also the implication of his creative approach to ethics. This has been legitimately called the Protestant Principle. It is simply a way of designating the demand that every dogmatism, every orthodoxy, every vested interest justify itself at the bar of love. That is, can it justify itself in terms of the public good? To exempt political and economic aspects of life from this question is to deny Jesus. This is not in line with his spirit. He was too aggressive in its application within the scope of his environment to permit us to act otherwise.

To go further than this in interpreting the mind of Jesus for our day invites arbitrariness or partisanship with reference to specific issues. Granting that, we can go further. Thinking in broad terms about our civilization, we can be sure that the spirit of Jesus speaks in philosophers of history who believe that spiritual and moral factors are determinative. Arnold J. Toynbee is one of these, an outstanding one. His study leads him to the conclusion that racial inheritance and environmental factors are not primary in the growth or decay of a civilization. Moral factors and decisions relative to them are primary. This is at least consistent with Jesus' insight reached on other grounds. This also stands over against the Greek cyclic view in its modern form, that, on the analogy of the seasons, a civilization is predetermined to pass through the stages of spring, summer, autumn, and winter.

Toynbee's more specific analysis of what happens in a disintegrating society like our own is also instructive. Four futile alternatives present themselves under such circumstances. The first is the effort to save the disintegrating society by establishing a dictatorship. A dominant minority rises to power by means of the sword. This was Hitler's way. It is Russia's way. It is what some white citizens in the United States want in order to keep the Negro "in his place." Others give up the effort to save their society. They seek escape from it along one of three lines. Some long for "the good old days," reconstructing them in imagination. They are the archaists. Everything would be all right, they think, if we could just turn the clock back. Others use their imagination in the same way, but with reference to the future. These futurists may be the Adventists with their apocalyptic dreams or they may be the utopians with their sights on this life. Still others detach themselves from all this in the form of philosophical speculation. They attempt to express their views through a ruler who entices the masses to accept the ideal form of government.

If history is any guide, says Toynbee, none of these succeeds. Under the pressure of circumstances the last three groups become disillusioned, and eventually turn to the sword to bring their dreams to pass. This is of no avail, because the sword carries within itself the seeds of its own destruction: "All who take the sword will perish by the sword." We are now in a position to feel the full force of that truth, at least with world war in mind.

Thus some other way, some creative way, must be found to renew the lifeblood of a society in process of decay. Toynbee points to that way as the historical manifestation of God's love in the Incarnate Son of God. Only as men are transfigured by that love can they hope for the fulfillment of the promise of their creation as sons of God. Only so can they survive at all. This is but to say in another way that Jesus' gospel of love has social implications. Grounded in faith in the God who is taking the initiative on every battle line, his servants fight for justice and peace. They fight not only for God in this way, but with him.

What is the meaning of this for the United States at the present time? What does it mean with reference especially to the power struggle the focus of which is the conflict between Russia and the West?

The genius of the United States lies in its Dream. It is essentially a Dream of a way of life free from tyranny, expressing itself in a form of government and in many practical ways. It is the age-old ideal of the Remnant, bearing God's purposes for mankind in spiritual and moral tones. The question for us is whether we are going to conceive of that as a Saved or a Saving Remnant. Are we going to interpret our good fortune and our capacity in terms of privilege or of responsibility to mankind? Due to the pressure of world events, we are at the crossroads now. Since 1945 we have been under terrific pressure to panic or to close our eyes to the real nature of our world. As one interpreter has well said, "Few people have ever been asked to enlarge their minds so fast, from the illusion of safety to the knowledge of danger." We now know that there is "no place to hide" from the challenge of a way of life that does not accept our assumptions, and is aggressively and cunningly propagated everywhere in the world. We now know that, militaristically speaking, we are no longer safe.

During the last fifteen years we have faltered. We permitted the Senator McCarthy nightmare. This was our attempt to run away from the facts of danger by seeking a scapegoat. There are those who would lead us still down that path. There are hopeful signs of an emerging maturity, however, that is outgrowing adolescence. After all, it was the people who cut McCarthy down. Once they saw what he was really doing on their television screens they wanted no part of him. The action of the Senate in censuring him followed that. In 1960 a magazine with national circulation ran a series of articles on our national purpose, to which over a thousand letters were received in response. The 1960 political campaign left much to be desired, but, in the midst of much obvious political maneuvering, there was, at least on the part of certain leaders, keen sensitivity to the present crisis of the nation and enlightened ideas about it.

It is mainly in the views of outstanding individuals that we hear the true accents of our Dream. One of these says that we do not need more clever schemes. We have these along with our vast resources. The need is for a mainspring to give drive to the pieces of the watch's mechanism, and this must be saturated with moral vision. Another says we are like a man in Chicago on his way to the coast who has stopped momentarily to decide which route to take. He knows where he wants to go, but he is uneasy because he has not yet made up his mind just how to do it. There is a moral flavor about the choices the different routes symbolize: the use of our wealth for public or private ends, the neglect or the beautification of our cities, research to the ends of profit or of cultural growth. To these other alternatives may be added: the treatment of the Negro as a second-class or as a first-class citizen; a foreign policy based upon a world that no longer exists or upon the real world of today; a calculated military risk or a calculated moral risk; in sum, quality or quantity.

The Dream still lives in the hearts of those who challenge us to the greatness that is ours by inheritance and that we must now win for ourselves. We can win it only by a convincing demonstration both at home and abroad. Lip service is of no avail. Self-righteousness but sickens and discourages our potential friends and all who need us in the world. Fear in the form of lazy thinking has already lost the prize. If the Dream is to be fulfilled, it must be paid for. It must be paid for in thought, in money, even in lives. We cannot remain in Midian when so many of our brothers are in desperate need and so confused as to what to do about it. We have the capacity for service, as in smaller compass Moses did, and that is in and of itself God's call to "Let my people go!" The call is for courage, for daring, in heart and mind. That is the challenge to the Saving Remnant.

The reason why we must accept this call is that God, as seen through Jesus, forces us to it. This is his redemptive enterprise interpreted in terms of world events. The Communist threat gives a certain urgency to all this, since survival is at stake. Survival means much more, however, than the perpetuation of physical or national existence. Unless we can survive spiritually and morally, nothing else is worth anything. Only by bringing its Dream to fulfillment can the United States survive in this sense. At root the Dream is a religious concept. It presupposes a conception of God derived from the Hebrew prophets and Jesus. Without that religious grounding in our experience we shall possess neither the insight nor the morale to fight, as we must, "without haste and without rest."

The genius of Jesus expresses itself most clearly on this point. The chief rivals to him today are not other great religious leaders and their followers. He is challenged primarily by half-gods or idols. They take the form of the worship of man. In essence this is what "scientism" means. It is also the meaning of the real religion of many people, that to which they are actually committed as being the greatest value. Communism for many of its devotees is such a religion. Nationalism, exalting the nation, is another virulent form that it takes. Jesus reveals to us the God who is the God of *all* men. He cannot be served by dedication of ourselves to less than the whole, except as a means to an end. Only as we cultivate his way of seeing the meaning of our existence can we bring all the separate parts of the Body into harmonious relationship. This is also the fundamental reason why the religion of Jesus is social, and social in the most inclusive terms. The God of love, whose love incorporates justice, calls us to fulfill his Dream for mankind. If we fail to heed his call, we shall pass into oblivion as surely as Nazi Germany has. If we do, the future is ours because it is God's. In either case the future will be on his terms. In that is both warning and hope. That at least is what Jesus challenges us to believe today.

We bring this study to a close by describing what is going on in one small segment of the social spectrum. It is an experiment with juvenile delinquency being conducted by a Harvard University psychologist in Cambridge, Massachusetts. The purpose of the experiment is not simply to gather clinical data. It is aimed at solving the problem of violence that flares forth in gang fights or "rumbles." Many people are involved in the form of teams that work together. Most of the participants are laymen without professional training in psychotherapy. One team approaches the youthful offenders directly. Its members seek them out on the street corners and the poolrooms where they hang out. They try to get them to discuss their outlook on life before a movie camera equipped with sound tape. Cooperation is secured at first by the offer of money, but later it is not needed. Following this stage come personal interviews with a trained psychotherapist. The experiment is still in its infancy, but already worth-while results are apparent. One of the most thrilling of these is the return of a reformed delinquent to his gang for the purpose of helping its members find what he has found. Having been one of them, he is more effective than the best trained professional. There are other experiments going on in other cities of the United States, with significant results.

Several observations might be made about this experiment as it bears upon the question of the social expression of religion. We confine ourselves to one point. If the religion of Jesus is to be relevant to our world, it must express itself in some such way as this with reference to every social dilemma. Assuming its religious motivation, from which comes its dynamic, it must face the problems squarely and work out ingeniously means and methods of dealing with them. It must be intensely practical. It must combine the best talents of professional and laymen. It must be willing to go where the needy are, and it must welcome into the fellowship the reformed individual so that his talents may also be enlisted in the enterprise. The problem of disarmament is not exactly the same as that of juvenile delinquency, but the basic principles apply in both directions.

The words of an old hymn come to mind:

> Jesus calls us: o'er the tumult
> Of our life's wild, restless sea,
> Day by day His sweet voice soundeth,
> Saying, "Christian, follow Me."

The words come with all the overtones that many of us associate with highly emotionalized revivals in which the emphasis was upon personal decision. There is no substitute for this decision, and no social legislation can be a substitute for personal integrity and good will. However, the call of Jesus comes not only in gentle terms, but, in the face of the world's need, it comes like the blast of a trumpet calling us to action. To follow him realistically is to be willing to face the hazards and the toil of working out practical solutions of pressing needs all along the line.

Looking back over the pages of this book, we are reminded that its purpose has been to interpret Jesus realistically and truly both in his ancient Palestinian setting and in his contemporary impact. This may or may not have been adequately done. At least we can understand why he has been called the Religious Ultimate. Confronting Jesus realistically and honestly, we come face to face with the God he served and revealed. Because of that we are enabled to see ourselves and our fellow men in true perspective. This brings forth our confession of faith that "there is no other name under heaven given among men by which we must be saved." Bearing witness to the power of this faith in our lives, inadequate though we be, God is able to use us in accomplishing his mighty redemptive purpose in human society. That this may be so, we pray (in words adapted from St. Paul): "*Maranatha*—Come, Lord Jesus!"

# BOOKS ON ANCIENT JUDAISM

❖❖❖❖❖❖❖ A very convenient selection of firsthand materials may be found in C. K. Barrett's *The New Testament Background: The Selected Documents* (New York, The Macmillan Company, 1957), especially Sections 1, 7, 8, 12. Introductory treatments of ancient Judaism include F. C. Grant's *Ancient Judaism and the New Testament* (New York, The Macmillan Company, 1959) and S. E. Johnson's *Jesus in His Homeland* (New York, Charles Scribner's Sons, 1957). More advanced studies include R. Bultmann's *Primitive Christianity in Its Contemporary Setting* (New York, Meridian Books, 1956), G. F. Moore's *Judaism in the First Centuries of the Christian Era* (Cambridge, Harvard University Press, 1927–1930), and R. H. Pfeiffer's *History of New Testament Times: With an Introduction to the Apocrypha* (New York, Harper & Brothers, 1949).